180 Days of Social-Emotional Learning
for First Grade

Kayse Hinrichsen, M.A.

Kris Hinrichsen, M.A.T., NBCT

Consultant

Amy Zoque
Teacher and Instructional Coach
Ontario Montclair School District

Publishing Credits

Corinne Burton, M.A.Ed., *Publisher*
Emily R. Smith, M.A.Ed., *VP of Content Development*
Lynette Ordoñez, *Content Specialist*
David Slayton, *Assistant Editor*
Jill Malcolm, *Multimedia Specialist*

Image Credits: all images from iStock and/or Shutterstock

Social-Emotional Learning Framework

The CASEL SEL framework and competencies were used in the development of this series.
© 2020 The Collaborative for Academic, Social, and Emotional Learning

A division of Teacher Created Materials
5482 Argosy Avenue
Huntington Beach, CA 92649-1039
www.tcmpub.com/shell-education
ISBN 978-1-0876-4970-2
© 2022 Shell Educational Publishing, Inc

Table of Contents

Introduction

"SEL is the process through which all young people and adults acquire and apply the knowledge, skills, and attitudes to develop healthy identities, manage emotions and achieve personal and collective goals, feel and show empathy for others, establish and maintain supportive relationships, and make responsible and caring decisions." (CASEL 2020)

Social-emotional learning (SEL) covers a wide range of skills that help people improve themselves and get fulfilment from their relationships. They are the skills that help propel us into the people we want to be. SEL skills give people the tools to think about the future and manage the day-to-day goal setting to get where we want to be.

The National Commission for Social, Emotional, and Academic Development (2018) noted that children need many skills, attitudes, and values to succeed in school, future careers, and life. "They require skills such as paying attention, setting goals, collaboration and planning for the future. They require attitudes such as internal motivation, perseverance, and a sense of purpose. They require values such as responsibility, honesty, and integrity. They require the abilities to think critically, consider different views, and problem solve." Explicit SEL instruction will help students develop and hone these important skills, attitudes, and values.

Daniel Goleman (2005), a social scientist who popularized SEL, adds, "Most of us have assumed that the kind of academic learning that goes on in school has little or nothing to do with one's emotions or social environment. Now, neuroscience is telling us exactly the opposite. The emotional centers of the brain are intricately interwoven with the neocortical areas involved in cognitive learning." As adults, we may find it difficult to focus on work after a bad day or a traumatic event. Similarly, student learning is impacted by their emotions. By teaching students how to deal with their emotions in a healthy way, they will reap the benefits academically as well.

SEL is doing the work to make sure students can be successful at home, with their friends, at school, in sports, in relationships, and in life. The skills are typically separated into five competencies: self-awareness, self-management, social awareness, relationship skills, and responsible decision-making.

Introduction *(cont.)*

Social-Emotional Competencies

SELF-MANAGEMENT
Manage your emotions, thoughts, and behaviors. Set and work toward goals.

SOCIAL AWARENESS
Take on the perspectives of others, especially those who are different from you. Understand societal expectations and know where to get support.

SELF-AWARENESS
Recognize your own emotions, thoughts, and values. Assess your strengths and weaknesses. Have a growth mindset.

RESPONSIBLE DECISION-MAKING
Make positive choices based on established norms. Understand and consider consequences.

RELATIONSHIP SKILLS
Establish and maintain relationships with others. Communicate effectively and negotiate conflict as necessary.

SEL COMPETENCIES

Each SEL competency helps support child development in life-long learning. SEL helps students develop the skills to have rich connections with their emotional lives and build robust emotional vocabularies. These competencies lead to some impressive data to support students being successful in school and in life.

- Students who learn SEL skills score an average of 11 percentage points higher on standardized tests.

- They are less likely to get office referrals and will spend more time in class.

- These students are more likely to want to come to school and report being happier while at school.

- Educators who teach SEL skills report a 77 percent increase in job satisfaction. (Durlack, et al. 2011)

Your SEL Skills

Educators, parents, and caretakers have a huge part to play as students develop SEL skills. Parker Palmer (2007) reminds us that what children do is often a reflection of what they see and experience. When you stay calm, name your feelings, practice clear communication, and problem-solve in a way that students see, then they reflect that modeling in their own relationships. As you guide students in how to handle conflicts, you can keep a growth mindset and know that with practice, your students can master any skill.

Scenarios

There are many benefits to teaching SEL, from how students behave at home to how they will succeed in life. Let's think about how children with strong SEL skills would react to common life experiences.

At Home

Kyle wakes up. He uses self-talk and says to himself, *I am going to do my best today.* He gets out of bed, picks out his own clothes to wear, and gets ready. As he sits down for breakfast, his little sister knocks over his glass of milk. He thinks, *Uggh, she is so messy! But that's ok—it was just an accident.* Then, he tells his parent and helps clean up the mess.

When his parent picks Kyle up from school, Kyle asks how they are feeling and answers questions about how his day has gone. He says that he found the reading lesson hard, but he used deep breathing and asked questions to figure out new words today.

As his family is getting dinner ready, he sees that his parent is making something he really doesn't like. He stomps his foot in protest, and then he goes to sit in his room for a while. When he comes out, he asks if they can make something tomorrow that he likes.

When he is getting ready for bed, he is silly and playful. He wants to read and point out how each person in the book is feeling. His parent asks him how he would handle the problem the character is facing, and then they talk about the situation.

At School

Cynthia gets to school a little late, and she has to check into the office. Cynthia is embarrassed about being late but feels safe at school and knows that the people there will welcome her with kindness. She steps into her room, and her class pauses to welcome her. Her teacher says, "I'm so glad you are here today."

Cynthia settles into her morning work. After a few minutes, she comes to a problem she doesn't know how to solve. After she gives it her best try, she asks her teacher for some help. Her teacher supports her learning, and Cynthia feels proud of herself for trying.

As lunchtime nears, Cynthia realizes she forgot her lunch in the car. She asks her teacher to call her mom. Her mom says she can't get away and that Cynthia is going to have to eat the school lunch today. Cynthia is frustrated but decides that she is not going to let it ruin her day.

As she is getting ready for school to end, her teacher invites the class to reflect about their day. What is something they are proud of? What is something they wished they could do again? Cynthia thinks about her answers and shares with the class.

These are both pretty dreamy children. The reality is that the development of SEL skills happens in different ways. Some days, students will shock you by how they handle a problem. Other times, they will dig in and not use the skills you teach them. One of the benefits of teaching SEL is that when a student is melting down, your mindset shifts to *I wonder how I can help them learn how to deal with this* rather than *I'm going to punish them so they don't do this again.* Viewing discipline as an opportunity to teach rather than punish is critical for students to learn SEL.

How to Use This Book

Using the Practice Pages

This series is designed to support the instruction of SEL. It is not a curriculum. The activities will help students practice, learn, and grow in their SEL skills. Each week is set up for students to practice all five SEL competencies.

 Day 1—Self-Awareness

 Day 2—Self-Management

 Day 3—Social Awareness

 Day 4—Relationship Skills

 Day 5—Responsible Decision-Making

Each of the five competencies has subcategories that are used to target specific skills each day. See the chart on pages 10–11 for a list of which skills are used throughout the book.

Each week also has a theme. These themes rotate and are repeated several times throughout the book. The following themes are included in this book:

- self
- friends
- family
- school
- neighborhood
- community

This book also features one week that focuses on online safety.

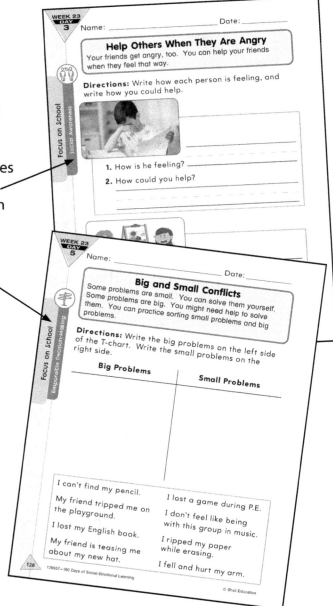

How to Use This Book *(cont.)*

Using the Resources

Rubrics for connecting to self, relating to others, and making decisions can be found on pages 198–200 and in the Digital Resources. Use the rubrics to consider student work. Be sure to share these rubrics with students so that they know what is expected of them.

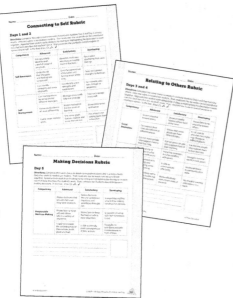

Diagnostic Assessment

Educators can use the pages in this book as diagnostic assessments. The data analysis tools included with this book enable teachers or parents/caregivers to quickly assess students' work and monitor their progress. Educators can quickly see which skills students may need to target further to develop proficiency.

Students will learn how to connect with their own emotions, how to connect with the emotions of others, and how to make good decisions. Assess student learning in each area using the rubrics on pages 198–200. Then, record their overall progress on the analysis sheets on pages 201–203. These charts are also provided in the Digital Resources as PDFs and Microsoft Excel® files.

To Complete the Analyses:

- Write or type students' names in the far-left column. Depending on the number of students, more than one copy of each form may be needed.

- The weeks in which students should be assessed are indicated in the first rows of the charts. Students should be assessed at the ends of those weeks.

- Review students' work for the day(s) indicated in the corresponding rubric. For example, if using the Making Decisions Analysis sheet for the first time, review students' work from Day 5 for all six weeks.

Integrating SEL into Your Teaching

Student self-assessment is key for SEL skills. If students can make accurate evaluations of how they are feeling, then they can work to manage their emotions. If they can manage their emotions, they are more likely to have better relationship skills and make responsible decisions. Children can self-assess from a very young age. The earlier you get them into this practice, the more they will use it and benefit from it for the rest of their lives. The following are some ways you can quickly and easily integrate student self-assessment into your daily routines.

Feelings Check-Ins

Using a scale can be helpful for a quick check-in. After an activity, ask students to rate how they are feeling. Focusing students' attention on how they are feeling helps support their self-awareness. Discuss how students' feelings change as they do different things. Provide students with a visual scale to support these check-ins. These could be taped to their desks or posted in your classroom. Full-color versions of the following scales can be found in the Digital Resources.

- **Emoji:** Having students point to different emoji faces is an easy way to use a rating scale with young students.

- **Symbols:** Symbols, such as weather icons, can also represent students' emotions.

- **Color Wheel:** A color wheel, where different colors represent different emotions, is another effective scale.

- **Numbers:** Have students show 1–5 fingers, with 5 being *I'm feeling great* to 1 being *I'm feeling awful*.

Integrating SEL into Your Teaching (cont.)

Reflection

Reflecting is the process of looking closely or deeply at something. When you prompt students with reflection questions, you are supporting this work. Here is a list of questions to get the reflection process started:

- What did you learn from this work?
- What are you proud of in this piece?
- What would you have done differently?
- What was the most challenging part?
- How could you improve this work?
- How did other people help you finish this work?
- How will doing your best on this assignment help you in the future?

Pan Balance

Have students hold out their arms on both sides of their bodies. Ask them a reflection question that has two possible answers. Students should respond by tipping one arm lower than the other (as if one side of the scale is heavier). Here are some example questions:

- Did you talk too much or too little?
- Were you distracted or engaged?
- Did you rush or take too much time?
- Did you stay calm or get angry?
- Was your response safe or unsafe?

Calibrating Student Assessments

Supporting student self-assessment means calibrating their thinking. You will have students who make mistakes but evaluate themselves as though they have never made a mistake in their lives. At the other end of the spectrum, you will likely see students who will be too hard on themselves. In both these cases, having a periodic calibration can help to support accuracy in their evaluations. The *Calibrating Student Assessments* chart is provided in the Digital Resources (calibrating.pdf).

Teaching Assessment

In addition to assessing students, consider the effectiveness of your own instruction. The *Teaching Rubric* can be found in the Digital Resources (teachingrubric.pdf). Use this tool to evaluate your SEL instruction. You may wish to complete this rubric at different points throughout the year to track your progress.

Skills Alignment

Each activity in this book is aligned to a CASEL competency. Within each competency, students will learn a variety of skills. Here are some of the important skills students will practice during the year.

 Self-Awareness

Identifying Emotions	Identifying Strengths
Cultural Identity	Examining Bias
Personal Identity	Staying Positive
Integrity	Dealing with Disappointment
Reflecting	Understanding Worry
Developing Interests	Role Models
Honesty	Mantras

Self-Management

Managing Emotions	Asking for Help
Calming Down	Understanding Triggers
Self-Talk	Dealing with Worry
Setting Goals	Kindness
Standing Up for Others	Bravery
Managing Stress	Accepting a Loss
Self-Control	

 Social Awareness

Considering Others' Feelings	Showing Concern for Others
Impact of One's Actions	Kindness
Gratitude	Noticing Dishonesty
Identifying Others' Strengths	Working with Others
Understanding Different Rules	Empathy
Fairness	Points of View
Predicting Others' Feelings	

Skills Alignment *(cont.)*

 Relationship Skills

Making Friends	Leadership
Listening Skills	Digital Communication
Body Language	Being Helpful
Standing Up for Yourself	Solving Conflicts
Being a Good Friend	Asking Questions
Communication Skills	Teamwork
Staying Safe	Apologizing
Understanding Culture	

 Responsible Decision-Making

Trying New Things	Forgiving Others
Solving Problems	Reflecting
Identifying Big and Small Problems	Dealing with Change
Understanding Consequences	Making Safe Choices
Making Good Choices	Critical Thinking
Helping Others	Impacts of Choices
Being Curious	Celebrating Success
Considering Choices	Pride

Name: _____ Date: _____

Know How You Feel

You have a lot of feelings. It is good to be able to name how you feel.

Directions: Look at each face. Write the feeling you see. Use words from the Word Bank.

Word Bank			
angry	happy	sad	scared

1.

_____

- - - - - - - - - - - - - - -

_____

3.

_____

- - - - - - - - - - - - - - -

_____

2.

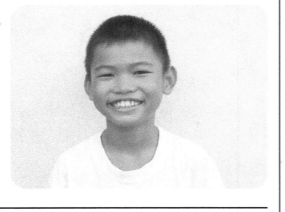

_____

- - - - - - - - - - - - - - -

_____

4.

_____

- - - - - - - - - - - - - - -

_____

126957—180 Days of Social-Emotional Learning

Calming Down

You can calm your body when you have big feelings. It is a skill you can learn.

Directions: Follow the steps with your breath. When the balloon is big, take a deep breath. Blow your air out slowly. When the balloon is empty, all your breath should be out. Do this a few times. Use these steps when you have big feelings.

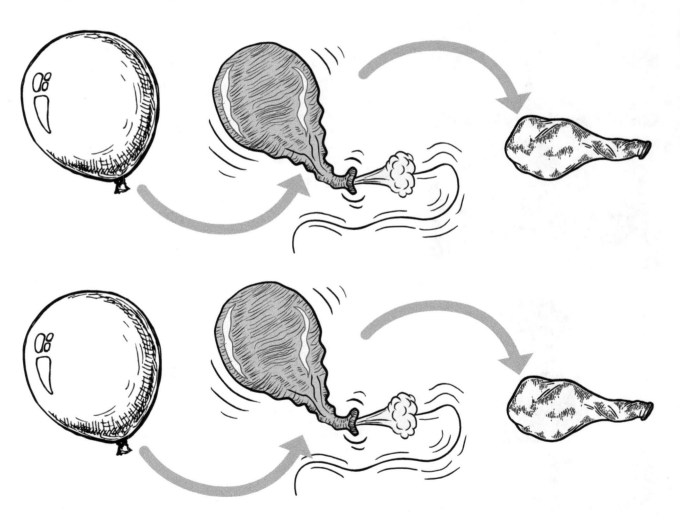

Name: _____ Date: _____

Thinking about Others' Feelings

You can see how other people feel. They will give you clues if you stop and notice.

Focus on Self

Social Awareness

Directions: Draw lines to match each picture with the right feeling.

Pictures	Feelings

angry

happy

sad

scared

Making Friends

It is fun to have friends.

Directions: Circle the pictures that show how to make a friend.

Focus on Self

Relationship Skills

Name: _____ Date: _____

Trying New Things
Trying new things can be a lot of fun.

Directions: Draw yourself trying something new.

Name: _____ Date: _____

Your Family

Families are made of all kinds of people.

Directions: Draw your family. Write their names.

My Family

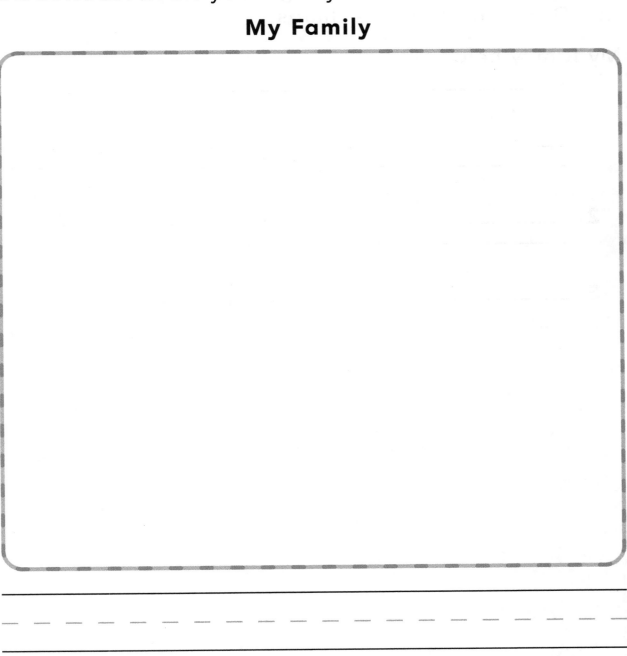

_____

- -

_____

_____

- -

_____

Focus on Family

Self-Awareness

Name: _____ Date: _____

Help from Your Family

Your family can help you do a lot of things.

Directions: Write three things your family helps you do. Draw one of those things.

My family helps me...

_____

1. _____

   _____

2. _____

   _____

3. _____

Name: _____ Date: _____

You Can Help!

You can help your family. It feels good to be a helper.

Directions: Color all the things you can do to help your family. Put a star by one you can do today.

Name: _____ Date: _____

Listen

You can show you care about your family. One way is to listen.

Directions: Match what the adult says with what should be done.

"Pick up your toys."

"Push in your chair."

"Close your door."

"Brush your teeth."

Name: _____ Date: _____

Problem-Solving

Your family will have problems. You can help solve them.

Directions: Draw what each person could do to help solve the problem.

Problem 1: Matt's sister hit him. What could Matt do?

Problem 2: Margo's mom spilled milk. What could Margo do?

Problem 3: Jack's brother takes Jack's toy. What could Jack do?

Responsible Decision-Making

Focus on Family

Name: _____ Date: _____

Name Your Feelings
Having good friends will help you feel good.

Directions: Draw one thing your friend does to make you feel good.

Self-Talk

When you get upset, you can talk to yourself to help calm down. This is called *self-talk*.

Directions: Color the self-talk bubbles that you could use when you are upset.

I can do this.

I can try again.

I am smart.

I will try my best.

I am a good friend.

I am learning.

Name: _____ Date: _____

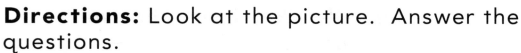

Your Friends' Feelings

You can watch your friends. You can see what they say and do. This will help you know how they feel.

Directions: Look at the picture. Answer the questions.

1. What is happening in the picture?

_____

- -

_____

_____

- -

_____

2. How might the friend in front feel?

_____

- -

_____

_____

- -

_____

Name: _____ Date: _____

Helping Others

It feels good to help others.

Directions: Look at each picture. Draw how you could help.

1.

2.

Name: _____ Date: _____

Big or Small Problems

Some problems with friends are big. You need an adult to help you solve them. Other problems are small. You can solve them on your own.

Directions: Circle to show if each problem is big or small.

1.

big problem

small problem

2.

big problem

small problem

3.

big problem

small problem

4.

big problem

small problem

Name: _____ Date: _____

Culture

Your culture includes a lot of things. It is where you live. It is what you eat. It can also be how you dress and how your family works.

Directions: Draw your family. Share your drawing with a partner. Then, answer the questions.

1. Are your families the same?

yes   no

2. Do you have the same number of people in your family?

yes   no

3. Are you wearing the same kinds of clothes?

yes   no

Name: _____ Date: _____

Managing Feelings

It is good to stay calm when you get upset. It can help to take a deep breath.

Directions: Look at each picture. Color the calm choice.

1.

2.

Name: _____ Date: _____

Friends

People in your community may look the same. They may act the same. They may look and act differently. They all have value.

Directions: Draw two friends from your community. Then, answer the questions.

Friend 1	Friend 2

1. How are these friends the same?

_____

_____

_____

2. How are they different?

_____

_____

_____

Name: _____ Date: _____

Homes
People can live in all kinds of homes.

Directions: Draw your home. Share your drawing with a partner. Then, answer the questions.

Focus on Community

Relationship Skills

1. How are your homes the same?

_____

- -

_____

_____

- -

_____

2. How are your homes different?

_____

- -

_____

_____

- -

_____

Try New Things

Your community has a lot of new things to try. You may like some. You may not like others.

Directions: Circle the things you would like to try.

Directions: Draw yourself doing one of the things you circled.

Focus on Community

Responsible Decision-Making

Name: _____ Date: _____

Identifying Emotions

It is helpful to know how you are feeling.

Directions: Circle the feeling word in each sentence. Use the Word Bank to help you.

Word Bank			
angry	love	sad	scared

1. I am very sad.

3. I am so angry with my dog.

2. I am scared of spiders.

4. I love my grandma.

Name: _____ Date: _____

Managing Feelings
Breathing can help you calm down.

Directions: Follow the steps to practice calm breathing. Then, answer the question.

Step 1: Breathe air in through your nose.

Step 2: Hold for five seconds.

Hold for
5, 4, 3, 2, 1.

Step 3: Breathe air out through your mouth.

1. How does breathing like this make you feel?

_____

_ _

_____

Name: _____ Date: _____

Focus on Self

Social Awareness

My Actions

Your actions matter. The things you do can make people feel happy or sad.

Directions: Draw a time when you made someone feel happy. Then, draw a time when you made someone feel sad.

Body Language

Communication is when you tell someone something. It is also when you listen. You can say things with words. Or you can use no words at all. You can use your body.

Directions: Write how each person is feeling. Then, circle the parts of their bodies that show their feelings.

_____

- -

1._____   2._____

Directions: Draw how your body looks when you are surprised.

Relationship Skills

Focus on Self

Name: _____ Date: _____

Solving Problems

You can help others. You can be a problem-solver.

Directions: Read the problem. Draw to show how Don and Hanna can solve it.

Painting Problem

Don and Hanna both want to paint. Don got the paints first, but Hanna has all the paintbrushes. What should they do?

Name: _____ Date: _____

Integrity

Integrity is doing the right thing. It means you do the right thing even when no one is watching.

Directions: Write what each person should say to do the right thing.

1.

_____
_ _ _ _ _ _ _ _ _ _ _ _ _ _ _ _ _
_____
_ _ _ _ _ _ _ _ _ _ _ _ _ _ _ _ _
_____
_ _ _ _ _ _ _ _ _ _ _ _ _ _ _ _ _
_____

2.

_ _ _ _ _ _ _ _ _ _ _ _ _ _ _ _ _
_____
_ _ _ _ _ _ _ _ _ _ _ _ _ _ _ _ _
_____
_ _ _ _ _ _ _ _ _ _ _ _ _ _ _ _ _

3.

_ _ _ _ _ _ _ _ _ _ _ _ _ _ _ _ _
_____
_ _ _ _ _ _ _ _ _ _ _ _ _ _ _ _ _
_____
_ _ _ _ _ _ _ _ _ _ _ _ _ _ _ _ _
_____

Name: _____ Date: _____

Set Goals

Working with your neighbors to set goals helps keep you safe. Start with a problem that needs to be solved.

Directions: Study the pictures. Write each neighborhood's problem.

1.

_____
_____
_____
_____
_____
_____
_____

2.

_____
_____
_____
_____
_____
_____
_____

3.

_____
_____
_____
_____
_____
_____

Say Thank You

You make others happy when you say thank you. It can make you feel happy, too. Small words can make a big difference.

Directions: Write how each person could say thank you.

1.

_____

– –

Thank you for _____.

2.

_____

– –

Thank you for _____.

3.

_____

– –

Thank you for _____.

Name: _____ Date: _____

Focus on Neighborhood

Relationship Skills

Culture

People celebrate a lot of things. Your neighbors may celebrate the same things. Or they may not. They may also celebrate the same things in different ways. There is no right or wrong way to celebrate.

Directions: Draw how your family celebrates a special event. Choose one event from the Word Bank, or choose your own.

Word Bank

birthday	New Year's Eve
Christmas	Ramadan
Hanukkah	Thanksgiving

Directions: Share your drawing with another person. Ask them how they celebrate a holiday.

Name: _____ Date: _____

Consequences

You can make good choices. Stop to think about what might happen when you do things.

Directions: Write what might happen because of each choice.

1.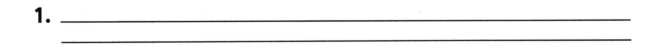

_____

_____

2. _____

_____

_____

Name: _____ Date: _____

Reflecting

When you think about things, you reflect. This can help you to get better.

Directions: Answer the questions. Then, draw what you learned.

1. What is something you learned at school?

_____

_____

_____

_____

2. How will you use this skill or knowledge?

_____

_____

_____

_____

Standing Up for Yourself and Others

It can be scary to stand up for yourself. It can be scary to stand up for others. But it is a brave thing to do.

Directions: Read the story. Write two things you can say to stand up for you and your friend. Be strong and kind.

Basketball Problem

You and your friend are playing basketball at school. Some other kids come up to you. They start making fun of you and your friend. You feel nervous. But you know what they are doing is not right. You know you need to say something.

_____

1. _____
_____
_____

2. _____
_____
_____
_____

Name: _____ Date: _____

Finding Strengths in Others

We all have strengths. Can you tell what other people are good at?

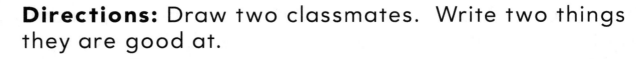

Focus on School

Social Awareness

Directions: Draw two classmates. Write two things they are good at.

Classmate 1

_____

- - - - - - - - - - - - - - - - - - - -

_____

- - - - - - - - - - - - - - - - - - - -

_____

- - - - - - - - - - - - - - - - - - - -

_____

- - - - - - - - - - - - - - - - - - - -

_____

Classmate 2

_____

- - - - - - - - - - - - - - - - - - - -

_____

- - - - - - - - - - - - - - - - - - - -

_____

- - - - - - - - - - - - - - - - - - - -

_____

- - - - - - - - - - - - - - - - - - - -

_____

Making Friends

It is important to have good friends. It feels good to be with nice people.

Directions: Imagine you are at a new school. You want to make new friends. Write two things you could do to meet nice people.

1. _____

_____

2. _____

_____

Directions: Draw a picture of you with a new friend.

Focus on School

Relationship Skills

Name: _____ Date: _____

Helping Others

You can help others. You can help make your school a great place by helping people there.

Directions: Answer the question. Draw yourself helping someone at your school.

1. What is one thing you can do to make your school a better place?

_____

- -

_____

_____

- -

_____

Name: _____ Date: _____

Know Your Interests

The things you enjoy doing are called your *interests*. They are how you spend your time.

Directions: Draw two of your interests. Pick one, and write why you love it.

_____

- -

_____

- -

_____

Name: _____ Date: _____

Standing Up
If someone is being mean to your friends, you can help.
You can stand up for your friends.

Directions: Write what you could say to help each friend.

1. _____
_____
_____
_____
_____
_____
_____

2. _____
_____
_____
_____
_____
_____
_____

3. _____
_____
_____
_____
_____
_____
_____

Name: _____ Date: _____

Rules

Rules keep us safe. Different places have their own rules.

Directions: Circle two things in each picture that are unsafe or against the rules.

126957—180 Days of Social-Emotional Learning

Name: _____ Date: _____

Focus on Community

Relationship Skills

Stand Up to Your Friends

Your friends may ask you to do something you don't want to do.

Directions: Match the response with the picture.

"It's not nice to make fun of people."

"We should not break things."

"That's stealing. I won't do that."

"You should not hurt people."

Name: _____ Date: _____

Being Grateful

It's good to think about all the good things you have.

Directions: Write three things in your community you are thankful for. Draw one of the things from your list.

I am thankful for...

_____

_____

_____

_____

Focus on Community

Responsible Decision-Making

Name: _____ Date: _____

Knowing What You Like

It is good to know what you like and what you do not like. This will help you do things that make you happy.

Directions: Circle the item you like best in each row. Or write your own choice.

Things I Like

dog   cat   _____
                          _ _ _ _ _ _ _ _ _ _ _ _ _
                          _____
                          _____

ocean   mountains   _ _ _ _ _ _ _ _ _ _ _ _ _
                          _____
                          _____
                          _ _ _ _ _ _ _ _ _ _ _ _ _

reading   drawing   _____

Directions: Write three things you do not like.

Things I Do Not Like

_____
_ _ _ _ _ _ _ _ _ _ _ _ _ _ _ _ _

1. Food: _____
_____

_ _ _ _ _ _ _ _ _ _ _ _ _ _ _ _ _

2. TV Show: _____
_____

_ _ _ _ _ _ _ _ _ _ _ _ _ _ _ _ _

3. Game: _____

How to Handle Big Feelings

We all have big feelings. You will be upset sometimes. It helps to know what to do when you feel that way. You can handle your big feelings.

Directions: Draw a time when you were upset. Draw another picture to show how you calmed yourself down.

Name: _____ Date: _____

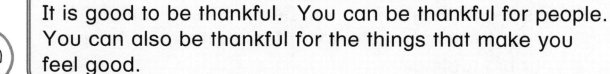

Being Thankful

It is good to be thankful. You can be thankful for people. You can also be thankful for the things that make you feel good.

Directions: Write the names of three people you are thankful for. Draw one of the people.

_____

_____

_____

_____

_____

_____

_____

© Shell Education

Focus on Self

Social Awareness

Name: _____ Date: _____

Being a Good Friend

Having good friends is a lot of fun. You need to be a good friend in order to have good friends.

Directions: Color the things that help you be a good friend. Then, draw someone who is a good friend to you.

funny	good sharer	nice
good listener	have a lot of toys	smart
happy	kind	talk a lot

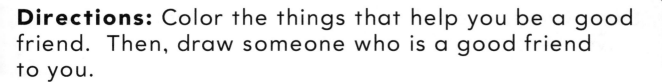

Relationship Skills

Focus on Self

Name: _____ Date: _____

Solving Problems

You can solve problems. It helps to think of two solutions. Then, choose the best one.

Directions: Read the problem. Write two ways to solve the problem.

The Game

Juan and Marcus are playing a game. They both want to go first. They start to argue. They can't start the game until they decide who gets to go first. How can Juan and Marcus solve this problem?

Solution 1

_____

_____

_____

_____

Solution 2

_____

_____

_____

_____

Be Honest

It can be hard to tell the truth. It is harder to tell the truth when you make a mistake. It is better to admit a mistake than to lie.

Directions: Draw lines from each mistake to the best apology.

> "I'm sorry. I ate the cake."

> "I'm sorry. I knocked over the beads."

> "I'm sorry. I threw the ball and broke the vase."

Name: _____ Date: _____

Help Your Family
You can find ways to help your family.

Focus on Family

Self-Management

Directions: Circle the things you can do to help your family.

clean my room   help cook dinner

make them laugh   pick up my toys

take out the trash   put away laundry

tell them I love them   wash dishes

Directions: Draw something you can do this week.

Name: _____ Date: _____

Say Thank You

Saying thank you is a kind thing to do.

Directions: Write a thank you note to someone in your family. Draw a picture for the person you thanked.

_____

Dear _____,

Thank you for _____
_____
_____.

It helps me feel _____
_____
_____.

Focus on Family

Social Awareness

Name: _____ Date: _____

Asking for Help

You will need help sometimes. Use kind words to ask for help. This will go a long way in getting what you need.

Directions: Write kind words each person could use to get help.

1. This girl needs help tying her shoes.

_____

_____

_____

_____

2. This girl can't reach the milk on the top shelf.

_____

_____

_____

_____

3. This boy needs help with homework.

_____

_____

_____

_____

126957—180 Days of Social-Emotional Learning

Consequences

Consequences are the results of the things you do. They can be good or bad.

Focus on Family

Responsible Decision-Making

Directions: Circle if each action will cause something good or something bad. Then, write your own action. Circle if its effect is good or bad, too.

1. Tyson helps his brother clean up their room.

good   bad

2. Ann gets ready for school on her own.

good   bad

3. Mark sits on his sister.

good   bad

4. Shelly rips her mom's work papers.

good   bad

5. _____

_____

_____

good   bad

Name: _____ Date: _____

Naming Your Emotions

To be a good friend, you need to learn more about who you are. Being a good friend starts with how you see yourself.

Directions: Finish the sentences about yourself.

1. My favorite thing to do is

_____

_____

_____.

2. I am really good at

_____

_____

_____.

3. I like to learn about

_____

_____

_____.

4. I am special because

_____

_____

_____.

Name: _____ Date: _____

Staying Calm under Pressure

It can be hard to stay calm when things are tense. You can calm your body. This will help keep you from getting out of control.

Directions: Read the story. Answer the question. Then, draw yourself calming down.

Focus on Friends

Self-Management

Getting Upset

Imagine you are playing with a friend. You get upset that they are not listening to you. You feel so mad. You want to yell.

1. What could you tell yourself to calm down?

_____

_____

_____

_____

Name: _____ Date: _____

Focus on Friends

Social Awareness

Your Actions Are Important
The things you say and do can affect others. Your actions can make people happy or sad.

Directions: Write the feeling that matches each action. Use the Word Bank to help you.

Word Bank		
angry	grateful	scared

1. You copy your friend's homework. You get caught. You both get a zero.

   _____

   Your friend feels _____ because of your actions.

2. You get really angry during a baseball game and throw down your bat near a group of friends.

   _____

   Your friends feel _____ because of your actions.

3. You find out your friend's grandma died. You bring flowers to their house with a card.

   _____

   Your friend feels _____ because of your actions.

Name: _____ Date: _____

Helping Others

It feels good to help others. It will help you build stronger friendships.

Directions: Draw a picture to show how you could help.

---

1. You see some trash on the ground.

---

2. Someone is playing alone.

---

3. A person drops a book.

---

4. Your friend doesn't have a partner for a game.

Name: _____ Date: _____

Finding Solutions

A conflict is a problem. You can help solve conflicts with friends.

Directions: Circle the best solution to each conflict. Then, draw a time you solved a problem.

Play with the ball together.

Take the ball, and run away.

Hide it in the corner.

Tell an adult, and try to make it better.

Name: _____ Date: _____

Helping Others

Your community has a lot of people. They work with each other. They help each other. You can help, too.

Directions: Match each problem with the place that can help. Then, color the place you think helps the most people.

Problems	Places

People don't have food to eat.

fire station

There is a fire.

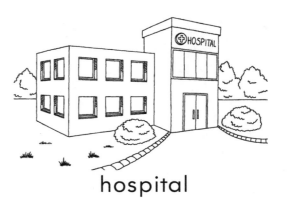

hospital

Someone is hurt.

food pantry

Name: _____ Date: _____

Calming Down

Things in your community might make you upset. It is good to know how to calm down. It can help to have a plan.

Directions: Say each number out loud as you color. When you feel mad, count from 10 to 1 to help you calm down.

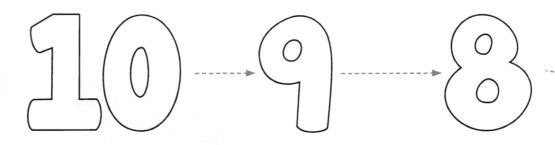

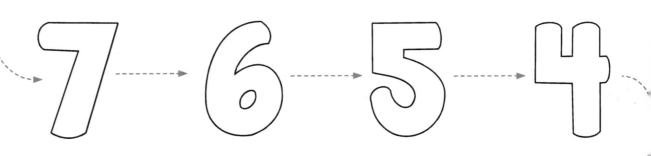

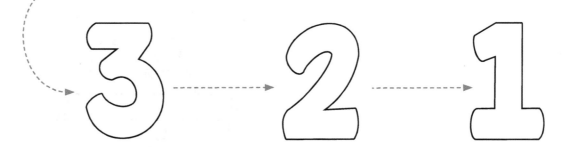

Name: _____ Date: _____

Fair and Unfair

Sometimes, rules might not seem fair. But rules are meant to keep us safe.

Directions: Answer the questions.

1. How does this sign keep you safe?

_____
_ _ _ _ _ _ _ _ _ _ _ _ _ _ _ _ _ _
_____
_____
_____

2. How does this sign keep you safe?

_____
_ _ _ _ _ _ _ _ _ _ _ _ _ _ _ _ _ _
_____
_____
_____

3. Is this rule fair? Why or why not?

_____
_ _ _ _ _ _ _ _ _ _ _ _ _ _ _ _ _ _
_____
_____
_____
_____

Name: _____ Date: _____

Finding Friends

You can make friends in your community. It helps to get out and do things.

Directions: Finish the sentences with words from the Word Bank.

Word Bank

| playing basketball | reading a book | taking a walk |

1. They are

_____

_ _ _ _ _ _ _ _ _ _ _ _ _ _ _ _ _ _ _ _

_____

_ _ _ _ _ _ _ _ _ _ _ _ _ _ _ _ _ _ _ _

_____.

2. They are

_____

_ _ _ _ _ _ _ _ _ _ _ _ _ _ _ _ _ _ _ _

_____

_ _ _ _ _ _ _ _ _ _ _ _ _ _ _ _ _ _ _ _

_____.

3. They are

_____

_ _ _ _ _ _ _ _ _ _ _ _ _ _ _ _ _ _ _ _

_____

_ _ _ _ _ _ _ _ _ _ _ _ _ _ _ _ _ _ _ _

_____.

Name: _____ Date: _____

Being Kind

Being kind helps people feel good. It can help you feel good, too.

Directions: Draw how you can be kind to each person.

1. You see someone drop a glove.

3. You see a friend fall down and get hurt.

2. Your best friend is running a long race.

4. You see someone sitting crying alone.

Focus on Community

Responsible Decision-Making

Name: _____ Date: _____

Focus on Self

Self-Awareness

Myself

How you see yourself is important. If you think you are kind, you are more likely to be kind. You can shape how you see yourself.

Directions: Draw a self-portrait. Then, write words that describe you around your picture.

Name: _____ Date: _____

Calming Down

You can help yourself feel more calm. One way is to think about your breathing. It can help you feel better when you are upset. This is a skill you can practice.

Directions: Follow the steps to practice box breathing. Repeat a few times. Then, draw your face to show how you feel.

Box Breathing

Count to four in your head while you breathe in. Then, count to four again while you hold your breath. Breathe out while counting to four. Then, count to four one last time before you breathe in again.

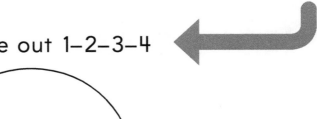

Breathe in 1–2–3–4

Hold 1–2–3–4   Hold 1–2–3–4

Breathe out 1–2–3–4

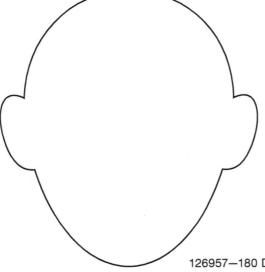

Self-Management

Focus on Self

Name: _____ Date: _____

Gratitude

Gratitude means being thankful. You can have gratitude for a person or a thing. It feels good to tell people you are thankful for them.

Directions: Finish the sentence about someone you are thankful for. Then, draw that person.

_____

- - - - - - - - - - - - - - - - - - -

I am thankful for _____

_____

- - - - - - - - - - - - - - - - - - -

because they _____.

Name: _____ Date: _____

Communication

You can communicate your feelings. You do not have to use words. You can use your body.

Directions: Draw how your body would look in each situation.

1. A dog runs up to you, barking.

2. You get a perfect score on a spelling test.

Relationship Skills

Focus on Self

Name: _____ Date: _____

You Can Help

You can help others. You may be young. But you can do something that is helpful.

Directions: Write the names of three people you know. Then, draw something you could do to help each person.

People I Know	How I Can Help
1. _____ _____	
2. _____ _____	
3. _____ _____	

Name: _____ Date: _____

Feelings Words

A lot of things happen in your neighborhood. Those things will give you a lot of feelings. It is good to talk about how you feel.

Directions: Finish each sentence with one of the feelings words.

angry	scared	excited	shy

 **1.** This person feels

_____

- - - - - - - - - - - - - - -

_____.

 **2.** This person feels

_____

- - - - - - - - - - - - - - -

_____.

 **3.** These people feel

_____

- - - - - - - - - - - - - - -

_____.

 **4.** These people feel

_____

- - - - - - - - - - - - - - -

_____.

Name: _____ Date: _____

Focus on Neighborhood

Self-Management

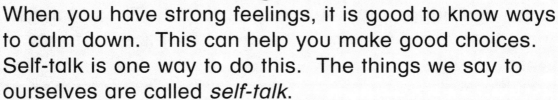

Using Self-Talk

When you have strong feelings, it is good to know ways to calm down. This can help you make good choices. Self-talk is one way to do this. The things we say to ourselves are called *self-talk*.

Directions: Connect each activity to the right self-talk. Then, draw one of the examples.

Your team loses a big game.	I'll be okay. There is other food I like.
The library is closed when you get there.	I'm sad we lost. It was really fun to play in the game.
There is a really long line at the store.	The library will be open another day.
They are out of the food you want for lunch.	I don't like waiting. But it won't be too long.

Name: _____ Date: _____

Predicting Feelings

You can predict how a person might feel. You may not always be right. But it is good to think about how others feel.

Directions: Write how each person might feel. Then, draw their face with that emotion.

1. Dawn has to wait at the stop sign. She is in a hurry.

   Dawn might feel

   _____

   _ _ _ _ _ _ _ _ _ _ _ _ _ _

   _____ .

2. Angel hits a big pothole on his bike. He falls off.

   Angel might feel

   _____

   _ _ _ _ _ _ _ _ _ _ _ _ _ _

   _____ .

3. Carlos's dad comes home from the army. He has been gone a long time.

   Carlos might feel

   _____

   _ _ _ _ _ _ _ _ _ _ _ _ _ _

   _____ .

Name: _____ Date: _____

Being Safe

You can do your part to protect your neighborhood. You can help keep it safe.

Focus on Neighborhood

Relationship Skills

Directions: Draw lines to match each sign with the right situation. Then, make your own sign.

| A new home is being built on your road. |

| People have seen bears in your neighborhood. |

| There is a crosswalk on a busy street. |

| Kids play in the street in your neighborhood. |

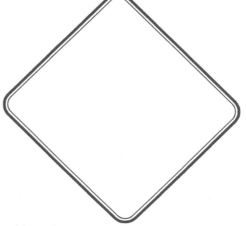

Name: _____ Date: _____

Making Good Choices

You can make good choices in your neighborhood. Your choices can help you and your neighbors feel safe.

Directions: Color one way you can make your neighborhood feel safe. Then, draw yourself doing it.

wear my helmet on my bike	say "Hello"	throw away my trash
keep my dog on a leash	watch out for cars	offer to help someone
follow the rules at the playground	invite someone to play	bake cookies for a neighbor
	help a neighbor rake leaves	

Name: _____ Date: _____

Focus on School

Self-Awareness

Your Identity

Your identity is how you think about yourself. It is how you act. It is who you are.

Directions: Color all the words that describe you.

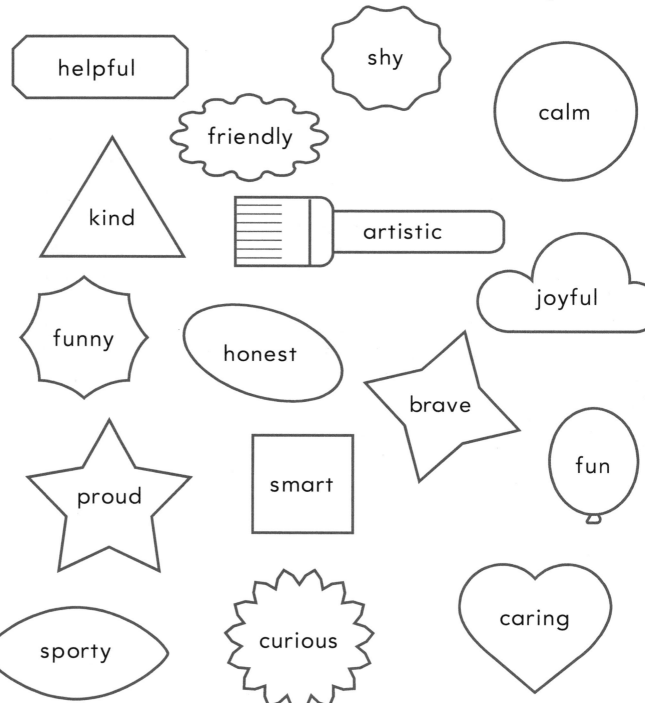

helpful

shy

calm

friendly

kind

artistic

joyful

funny

honest

brave

proud

smart

fun

sporty

curious

caring

Feeling Calm

We all get nervous at school. You can find ways to calm your body. This will help you focus.

Directions: Draw a picture to show what you do when you are nervous at school.

Draw something at school that makes you nervous.

Draw what you do to calm down and focus.

Draw how you feel after you calm down.

Focus on School

Self-Management

Name: _____ Date: _____

Showing Concern for Others

Being kind to others feels good. You can help people feel better. You can help when they are having a tough day.

Directions: Write one thing you could do for each person to help them feel better.

1. _____

2. _____

Name: _____ Date: _____

Communication

Communication has two parts. One person talks. The other person listens. Being a good listener takes work. You can get better with practice.

Directions: Read the ways to be a good listener. Color each step as you go. Circle the one that is hardest for you.

1. Keep your eyes on the speaker.

2. Keep your ears listening.

3. Keep your mouth closed so you don't interrupt.

4. Keep your body calm.

5. Keep your mind engaged so you can think about what the person is saying.

Name: _____ Date: _____

Solve Problems

Big and small problems happen at school. You need an adult to help you solve big problems. But you can solve small problems on your own.

Directions: Write an *X* to show if each problem is big or small.

Big Problem		Small Problem
	Ron takes your pencil.	
	You see smoke coming from a computer.	
	Mayra falls and breaks her foot.	
	Aimee is thirsty.	
	Julio takes food from your lunch.	

Directions: Draw yourself solving one of the small problems.

Name: _____ Date: _____

Staying Calm

Life can get really busy. It can help to stop and calm your body and mind.

Directions: Check one thing from the list that might annoy you. Then, draw how you can calm your body and mind.

Focus on Community

Self-Awareness

☐ You are going to see a movie, but the theater is closed.

☐ The store is out of the shirt you really wanted to buy.

☐ A person bumps into you in a restaurant, and you spill your food.

☐ You show up to a party in the same shirt as someone else.

☐ Your parent forgets where the car is parked.

☐ You go to a professional sports game, but your team loses.

Name: _____ Date: _____

Stress

Stress is when you worry about something. Stress can make you angry. It can make you scared or tired. Or it can make your stomach hurt.

Directions: Write how each student's body shows they are stressed.

_____

_____

Eyes: _____

Eyes: _____

_____

_____

Mouth: _____

Mouth: _____

_____

_____

Hands: _____

Hands: _____

Directions: Think about how your body feels when you are stressed. Write three things that happen.

_____

1. _____

_____

2. _____

_____

3. _____

 126957—180 Days of Social-Emotional Learning

Name: _____ Date: _____

Being Thankful

Other people can help us deal with our stress. It is a good idea to thank them for their help.

Directions: Write a thank you statement for each example.

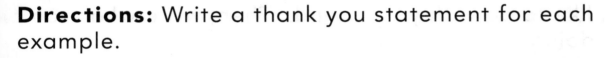

You are running late to a baseball game. Your friend saves you a spot.

_____

Thank you for _____

_____

_____

_____

_____ .

You bump a stack of boxes in a store. They all fall. Your brother helps you restack them.

_____

Thank you for _____

_____

_____

_____

_____ .

Focus on Community

Social Awareness

Name: _____ Date: _____

Making Good Friends
Spending time with friends can help you feel less stressed.

Focus on Community

Relationship Skills

Directions: Write a friend's name. Draw something you like to do with your friend. Then, write what you are doing.

_____
- -

My friend's name is _____.

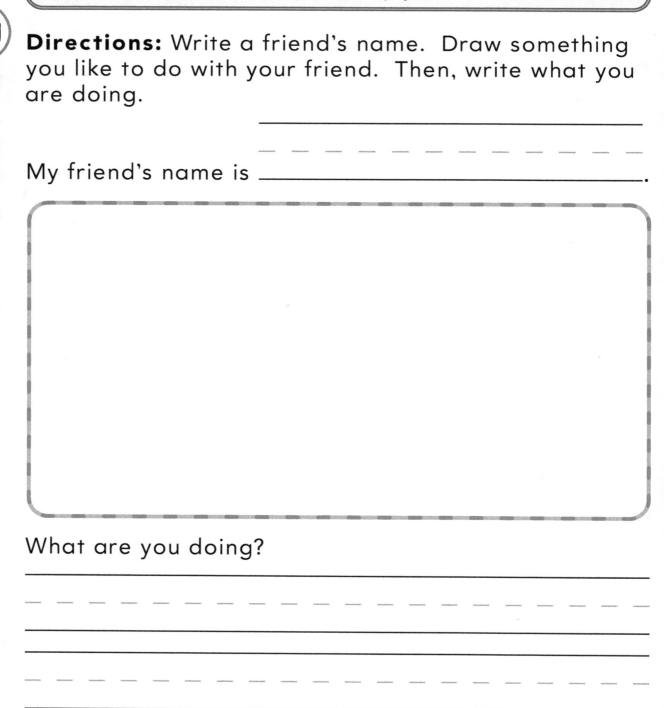

What are you doing?

_____

_____

_____

_____

_____

Name: _____ Date: _____

Help Your Community

You can have fun and still be safe. This will help all people in your community.

Focus on Community

Responsible Decision-Making

Directions: Circle if each person looks stressed or calm.

1.

stressed

calm

2.

stressed

calm

Directions: Think about how you would feel for each activity. Write an **S** for stressed and a **C** for calm.

3. riding a roller coaster _____

4. swimming at the beach _____

5. shopping in a crowded place _____

6. playing basketball on a team _____

Name: _____ Date: _____

Focus on Self

Self-Awareness

I Am Good At...

Everyone is good at something. You are good at a lot of things. Knowing what you are good at helps you have fun.

Directions: Draw one thing you are good at in each of the places.

School

Home

Outside

Name: _____ Date: _____

Setting Goals

Setting goals helps you get things done. Take small steps to a goal. Before long, you will finish.

Directions: Choose one goal from the list. Write your goal and the steps you will take to reach it.

tie my shoes

make a basket

read by myself

Focus on Self

Self-Management

_____

My Goal: _____

_____

Step 1: _____

_____

Step 2: _____

_____

Step 3: _____

Name: _____ Date: _____

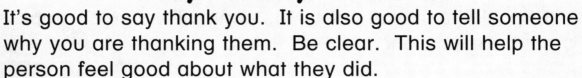

Ways to Say Thank You

It's good to say thank you. It is also good to tell someone why you are thanking them. Be clear. This will help the person feel good about what they did.

Focus on Self

Social Awareness

Directions: Write a thank you for each person. Follow the example.

Example

Kent's mom made his favorite breakfast, blueberry pancakes.

Thank you for making pancakes.

1. Kelsey's brother helped her clean up a big mess.

_____
_____
_____
_____

2. Gracie's cousin asked her to come over and play.

_____
_____
_____
_____

Name: _____ Date: _____

My Culture

Your culture is special. It is one thing that makes you who you are. Families celebrate special days. It is part of their cultures.

Directions: Answer the questions about what you do on your birthday. Or choose a different special day.

1. Who do you spend time with?

_____

- -

_____

2. What do you eat?

_____

- -

_____

3. Draw how you spend the day.

Name: _____ Date: _____

Being Curious

When you are curious, you think about things you want to learn. You want to know more. This can help you find things you like.

Directions: Write three things you are curious about. Draw a star next to one. Ask a friend or an adult to tell you one fact about it. Or look up a fact about it in a book or on online. Write what you learned.

1. I am curious about
_____

_ _ _ _ _ _ _ _ _ _ _ _ _ _ _ _ _ _

_____.

2. I am curious about
_____

_ _ _ _ _ _ _ _ _ _ _ _ _ _ _ _ _ _

_____.

3. I am curious about
_____

_ _ _ _ _ _ _ _ _ _ _ _ _ _ _ _ _ _

_____

_ _ _ _ _ _ _ _ _ _ _ _ _ _ _ _ _ _

4. I learned: _____
_____

_ _ _ _ _ _ _ _ _ _ _ _ _ _ _ _ _ _

_____

_____

_ _ _ _ _ _ _ _ _ _ _ _ _ _ _ _ _ _

_____.

Name: _____ Date: _____

Feelings Connected to Actions

How you feel can change how you act. Think about how you feel. This can help you get ready to do hard things.

Directions: How would you feel about each of these hard things? Draw a picture.

learning how to swim	building a model plane
learning a new language	learning how to play a musical instrument

Name: _____ Date: _____

Focus on Family

Self-Management

Controlling Your Actions

Thinking you can do something is the first step in doing hard things. You can do hard things!

Directions: Write what you could think to get started on each hard job.

1. To get started cleaning my room, I could think

_____
_____
_____
_____
_____.

2. To get started solving this puzzle, I could think

_____
_____
_____
_____.

3. To get started cleaning up after dinner, I could think

_____
_____
_____
_____.

Name: _____ Date: _____

Your Family's Feelings

Think about your family's feelings. It will make them feel good. It shows you care.

Directions: Draw how each action would make your family feel.

1. You made them a snack.

3. You read to them.

2. You cleaned up your mess.

4. You helped put away groceries.

Focus on Family

Social Awareness

Name: _____ Date: _____

Helping Your Family

Take time to help your family. It will make them happy. It will help you be happy, too.

Directions: Write how each person is helping their family. Then, answer the question.

1. They are helping by

_____

_ _ _ _ _ _ _ _ _ _ _ _ _ _ _

_____.

2. They are helping by

_____

_ _ _ _ _ _ _ _ _ _ _ _ _ _ _

_____.

3. They are helping by

_____

_ _ _ _ _ _ _ _ _ _ _ _ _ _ _

_____.

4. How could you help your family today?

_____

_ _

_____

_____

_ _

_____

Name: _____ Date: _____

Your Family Shapes Your Thinking

Your family shapes the way you think. This can affect the way you treat others.

Directions: Write what your family would do in each situation.

1. My family would

_____

_____

_____

_____.

2. My family would

_____

_____

_____

_____.

3. My family would

_____

_____

_____

_____.

Name: _____ Date: _____

Focus on Friends

Self-Awareness

I-Messages

An I-message is a way to help solve problems. They help you tell others how you are feeling. They tell people what you wish would happen, too.

Directions: Fill in the feeling part of each I-message.

1. I feel _____
(feeling)

    when <u>you spill paint on my picture.</u> Next time,
    (what they did)

    please <u>be more careful.</u>
    (what you want them to do)

2. I feel _____
(feeling)

    when <u>you take my crayons.</u> Next time, please
    (what they did)

    <u>ask before you use my things.</u>
    (what you want them to do)

3. I feel _____
(feeling)

    when <u>you don't include me.</u> Next time, please
    (what they did)

    <u>ask if I would like to play.</u>
    (what you want them to do)

I-Messages

To use an I-message, you need to know why something bothers you. This is the *when* part.

Directions: Fill in the reason each person is upset.

1. Lee and Izzy are reading a book together. Izzy is hogging the book, and Lee can't see it very well. Lee feels annoyed when Izzy...

   (A) wants to read with someone else.

   (B) blocks the book so he can't see.

2. Hazel is trying to finish writing a story. Fatima wants to talk about the movie she saw this weekend. Hazel feels frustrated when Fatima...

   (A) talks to her when she is writing.

   (B) goes to the movies without her.

Directions: Draw one of the problems above.

Name: _____ Date: _____

I-Messages

An I-message is a way to help solve problems. Conflicts have two or more people. It's helpful to think about people's feelings. This is called *empathy*.

Focus on Friends — Social Awareness

Directions: Read each story. Answer the questions.

Kent and Jackson are riding bikes. Kent loses control and runs into Jackson. Both boys fall and scrape their knees.

1. How is Kent feeling?

_____

- - - - - - - - - - - - - - - -

_____

2. How is Jackson feeling?

_____

- - - - - - - - - - - - - - - -

_____

June and Renee are playing a game. June is winning. Renee thinks she must be cheating. Renee yells at June to play fair.

3. How is June feeling?

_____

- - - - - - - - - - - - - - - -

_____

4. How is Renee feeling?

_____

- - - - - - - - - - - - - - - -

_____

Name: _____ Date: _____

I-Messages

An I-message is a way to help solve problems. You should use a strong voice. Don't yell or whisper, but be confident.

Directions: Read the I-messages. Then, help rewrite them.

Focus on Friends

Relationship Skills

Justin yells to Stephanie:

I feel <u>so mad</u> when <u>you steal my snack!</u> Next time, <u>I'm going to hurt you!</u>

How could Justin fix his I-message?

_____   _____
_ _

I feel _____ when _____.
                                   _____
                         _ _ _ _ _ _ _ _ _ _ _ _ _ _ _ _

Next time, will you _____?

Jose yells to Huck:

I feel <u>so angry</u> when <u>you rip my picture!</u> Next time, <u>I'm going to color on your paper!</u>

How could Jose fix his I-message?

_____   _____
_ _

I feel _____ when _____.
                                   _____
                         _ _ _ _ _ _ _ _ _ _ _ _ _ _ _ _

Next time, will you _____?

Name: _____ Date: _____

I-Messages

An I-message is a way to help solve problems. But there are times when an I-message won't work. They work best if you know the person well.

Directions: Circle whether each person should use an I-message.

1. Ronnie just met Josh at a camp. Josh moved Ronnie's bag over to a different bed so that Josh could be next to his friend.   yes   no

··

2. Leo's best friend, Ryan, just took a ball Leo was playing with.   yes   no

··

3. Aaron grew up next to Andrew, and they have been friends for years. Aaron took Andrew's phone without asking.   yes   no

··

4. Leslie and Tam met last week. Leslie invited Tam over to play. While they were playing, Tam was rough with Leslie's toys.   yes   no

Know Your Feelings

Trying new things can be hard. You may feel like you are not very good. That can be embarrassing. You might want to give up.

Directions: Write how each person shows that they are embarrassed. Look at their faces and bodies.

1. _____
_____
_____
_____
_____
_____

2. _____
_____
_____
_____
_____
_____

Name: _____ Date: _____

Asking for Help

When something is really hard, you can ask an adult to help you. You might need to practice how to ask. You can practice the words you will use. You can practice when you will ask.

Directions: Match each problem with the way to ask for help.

Kaylee is having trouble tying her shoes.	"Can you help me find a book about bears?"
Josh is having trouble hitting the ball in tennis.	"Can you help me learn how to make a basket?"
Julian is having trouble finding a book he wants to read.	"Can you teach me how to tie my shoes?"
Ayanna is having trouble making a basket.	"Can you show me how to hit the tennis ball?"

Name: _____ Date: _____

Seeing Others' Strengths

Good friends notice what others are good at. They share nice words to celebrate their friends.

Directions: Write and draw about a friend.

My friend's name is:

_____

- -

_____

They are good at:

_____

- -

_____

This is a picture of my friend.

Focus on Community

Social Awareness

Name: _____ Date: _____

Being a Leader

A leader is a person who helps others. They work hard to find ways to help.

Directions: Write how each person is being a good leader.

1. _____
_____
_____
_____

2. _____
_____
_____
_____

3. _____
_____
_____
_____

Name: _____ Date: _____

Solving Problems

Laws are made to solve problems. Laws also keep people safe. Signs help people remember the laws.

Directions: Write the problem that each sign helps solve. Then, write how it keeps you safe.

WEAR SEAT BELTS

1. Problem: _____
_____
_____
_____

2. This keeps me safe by
_____
_____
_____
_____
_____.

3. Problem: _____
_____
_____

4. This keeps me safe by
_____
_____
_____
_____
_____.

Name: _____ Date: _____

Be Honest

Using technology can be a lot of fun. But it is good to have rules to stay safe. Adults set rules for how to use these things to make sure you stay safe. It is important for you to follow these rules.

Directions: Draw stars next to the rules that are easy to follow. Write **X**s next to the rules that are hard to follow.

Computer Rules

Use two hands when you are carrying a computer.

Do not eat food or drink around your device.

Press keys lightly.

Do not spend too much time in front of a screen.

Only use the programs you are allowed to.

Charge your device when you are done so it's ready for next time.

Be kind to others while online.

Ask for Help

Things can go wrong when you use a device. You might need to ask for help.

Directions: Circle the things you would need to ask for help with.

Directions: Choose one thing you circled. Finish the sentence.

Can you please help me

_____

_ _ _ _ _ _ _ _ _ _ _ _ _ _ _ _ _ _

_____

_ _ _ _ _ _ _ _ _ _ _ _ _ _ _ _ _ _

_____?

Name: _____ Date: _____

Be Kind to Others

Some games and apps let you talk to other people. Sometimes, those people are your friends. Other times, they are strangers. Be kind with your words online. And stay safe.

Directions: Match each statement with the words or actions that go with it. Then, draw one way to stay safe online.

Someone beats you in a game.	Delete and ignore messages from strangers.
Your friend hurts your feelings.	"Nice game. Let's play again."
Someone you don't know tries to message you.	"What you said really hurt my feelings."

Name: _____ Date: _____

Digital Communication

People use shortened words or phrases when they text. It can be confusing. You may not know what they mean.

Directions: Write what the texts and images mean. You may need to ask an adult or look them up. Then, write and draw your own.

_____

1. lol _____

_____

2. brb _____

_____

3. _____

_____

4. _____

_____

5. My Text: _____

6. My Emoji:

Directions: Share your text and emoji with a friend. See if they can figure out your codes.

Name: _____ Date: _____

Consider Your Actions

The things you do lead to consequences. That is true on devices, too. Not following the rules can cause problems. Choose to be safe.

Directions: Look at the picture. Answer the question. Then, draw what you could do to make sure this accident does not happen.

1. What might happen to the computer?

_____

- -

_____

_____

- -

_____

Name: _____ Date: _____

Examining Bias

There are a lot of things that are the same about people.
There are a lot of things that are not the same.

Directions: Choose two homes. Then, write what is the same and what is different.

Home 1 **Home 2** **Home 3** **Home 4**

Things That Are the Same

_____

_____

_____

_____

_____

Things That Are Different

_____

_____

_____

_____

_____

Name: _____ Date: _____

Standing Up for Others

People can say and do mean things. This can hurt other people's feelings. You can be a good friend by standing up for your friends.

Directions: Draw what you would do to stand up for your friends.

1. Your friend was not invited to a birthday party.

2. Your friend is being made fun of for wearing glasses.

Name: _____ Date: _____

Thinking about Others' Feelings

Your neighbors might be different from you. They may not act the same way. They may not wear the same clothes. They may show feelings in a different way. They are still your neighbors.

Directions: Color the pictures. Answer the question.

1. Does your family look like one of these families? Explain.

_____

- -

_____

_____

- -

_____

Name: _____ Date: _____

Offering to Help Others

You can offer to help your neighbors.

Focus on Neighborhood

Relationship Skills

Directions: Draw a star next to two things you can do to help your neighbors. Then, answer the questions.

Let them borrow some food.

Make them some cookies.

Offer to walk their dog.

Offer to clean their car.

Make them a card.

Offer to play with them.

Invite them over for dinner.

Go on a walk with them.

1. How will your neighbors feel?

_____

_____

2. How will you feel?

_____

_____

Saying Sorry

Sometimes, we make mistakes. We have to say sorry. It feels good to make things right.

Directions: Finish each picture with an apology.

I'm sorry for

I'm sorry for

Name: _____ Date: _____

Know How You Feel

It is OK to be angry. You can feel a little angry, or you can be very angry. But it helps to know how you feel.

Directions: Put the anger words in order from a little angry to very angry. Then, draw how your face looks when it is a little angry and when it is very angry.

annoyed	furious	mad
frustrated	irritated	

Very Angry

_____

_____

_____

_____

_____

_____

_____

_____

A Little Angry

Very Angry

A Little Angry

Name: _____ Date: _____

Calming Down

You will get angry at school. Knowing what that feels like will help you make good choices. It will help you calm down. Then, you can think clearly.

Directions: Draw your classroom or learning space. Then, follow the steps to add more details.

1. Circle a place where you can go if you need a quiet space.

2. Draw a box around a place where you can talk to a friend.

3. Draw a star by a place where you can move your body.

4. Draw a triangle around a place where you can find help with your work.

Name: _____ Date: _____

Focus on School

Social Awareness

Help Others When They Are Angry

Your friends get angry, too. You can help your friends when they feel that way.

Directions: Write how each person is feeling, and write how you could help.

_____

_____

1. How is he feeling? _____

2. How could you help?

_____

_____

_____

_____

_____

3. How are they feeling? _____

4. How could you help?

_____

_____

_____

Name: _____ Date: _____

Solving Conflicts

It can be hard to solve a conflict when people are angry. It can be hard to think when you feel that way. It can help to practice.

Directions: Complete and practice each problem.

Your best friend falls down on the playground. You start to laugh. Your friend gets angry.

Find a friend or stuffed animal, and practice this apology: "I'm sorry I laughed at you when you fell. Are you okay? Is there anything I can do to help you?"

You and your friend are painting in class. You reach for another color. But you accidentally spill paint onto your friend's painting. Your friend is upset.

Write what you could say to your friend.

_____

_____

_____

_____

_____

_____

Relationship Skills

Focus on School

Name: _____ Date: _____

Focus on School

Responsible Decision-Making

Big and Small Problems

Some problems are small. You can solve them yourself. Some problems are big. You might need help to solve them. You can practice sorting small problems and big problems.

Directions: Write the big problems on the left side of the T-chart. Write the small problems on the right side.

Big Problems	Small Problems

I can't find my pencil.   I lost a game.

My friend tripped me.   I don't feel like singing.

I lost my book.   I ripped my paper.

My friend is teasing me.   I fell and hurt my arm.

 126957—180 Days of Social-Emotional Learning

Name: _____ Date: _____

Connecting Feelings to Actions
When you know how you feel, you can find things you like. You can also avoid things you don't like.

Directions: Look at the pictures. Answer the questions.

1. How does this person feel?

_____

- - - - - - - - - - - - - - - - - - - -

_____

2. How can you tell?

_____

- - - - - - - - - - - - - - - - - - - -

_____

_____

_____

3. How does this person feel?

_____

- - - - - - - - - - - - - - - - - - - -

_____

4. How can you tell?

_____

- - - - - - - - - - - - - - - - - - - -

_____

_____

- - - - - - - - - - - - - - - - - - - -

_____

Focus on Community

Self-Awareness

Name: _____ Date: _____

Focus on Community

Self-Management

Know Your Triggers

A trigger is a thing that makes you mad. It is good to know what your triggers are.

Directions: Draw something that could trigger you in your community. Use an example from the list, or choose your own. Then, answer the questions.

waiting in a long line	being in a crowded place
being late to a movie	not being able to buy something

1. What is your trigger?

_____

_____

2. How does it make you act?

_____

_____

_____

_____

Name: _____ Date: _____

Showing Concern for Others

Other people have triggers, too. It can be confusing if their triggers are not the same as yours. You may not know why they are mad. If you stay calm, you can help the problem stay small.

Directions: Imagine what might have happened to each person before they got mad. Write their thoughts in the pictures.

1. Juan shows up to practice and is very upset.

2. Sofia is at the museum. She does not look happy.

Name: _____ Date: _____

Standing Up for Others

It is frustrating when others are not treated fairly. It can trigger you. You can stand up for others. An adult could help. It takes courage to help a friend.

Directions: Read the story. Answer the questions.

Ed really loves to dance. The teacher says dance is for girls only.

_____

_____

1. What is unfair? _____
_____

_____

2. What could you say to an adult to help fix what is unfair?
_____

_____

_____

_____

_____

Name: _____ Date: _____

Find a Way to Help

First graders all over the world are finding ways to help others. You can help, too. You can help in your own community.

Directions: Read each story. Answer the questions.

Recycling

Ryan has been recycling since he was three. Now, he collects bottles and cans from his neighbors. He takes them to be recycled.

1. How is Ryan changing the world?

_____

_ _ _ _ _ _ _ _ _ _ _ _ _ _ _ _ _ _ _

_____

_ _ _ _ _ _ _ _ _ _ _ _ _ _ _ _ _ _ _

_____

Shoes

Jess helps kids in need get new shoes. She collects money from neighbors. Then, she buys shoes and gives them to kids who don't have shoes.

2. How is Jess changing the world?

_____

_ _ _ _ _ _ _ _ _ _ _ _ _ _ _ _ _ _ _

_____

_ _ _ _ _ _ _ _ _ _ _ _ _ _ _ _ _ _ _

_____

Name: _____ Date: _____

Focus on Self

Self-Awareness

Think Positive Thoughts

Your brain is like a muscle. You can work to make your brain stronger. Thinking positive thoughts is one way.

Directions: Color the balloons that have positive thoughts you would like to have.

I am amazing.

I am proud of myself.

I can get through this.

I will try my best.

I can do this.

I can do hard things.

I am smart.

Directions: Write your three favorite thoughts you colored. Say them three times a day.

1. _____

2. _____

3. _____

Name: _____ Date: _____

Helping Others Helps You

It feels good to help other people. It can help you feel good, too.

Directions: Write four ways you could help your friends and family. Draw one of your ideas.

Name: _____ Date: _____

Focus on Self

Social Awareness

Positive Messages for Others

Writing notes to other people is a kind thing to do. It is one way to thank people. It can make people feel really good.

Directions: Circle a message you would like to write to someone else. Write who it is for.

You are a great friend.

You are important to me.

You are really fun.

You matter to me.

You are smart.

You can do this.

You are strong.

You can do hard things.

You are kind.

You are doing a great job.

1. Who is this for?

_____

_____

_____

Directions: Make a card for the person you chose. Write your message in the card. Decorate your card. Give it to the person.

Name: _____ Date: _____

Ask Questions

You probably know a lot about your friends. You can ask questions to learn more.

Directions: Ask a friend each question. Draw their answers.

1. What is your favorite thing to do?

3. Would you rather be able to fly or be invisible? Why?

2. What is your favorite place to eat?

4. What is your favorite TV show?

Relationship Skills

Focus on Self

Name: _____ Date: _____

Focus on Self

Responsible Decision-Making

Think through Your Choices

Sometimes, you have to make hard choices. You can make a good choice by taking a break. You can stop and think before you act.

Directions: Fill in the best choice.

1.

I don't like the food at my friend's house. I should...

Ⓐ call my family to come get me.

Ⓑ tell them the food is gross and I don't like it.

Ⓒ try to eat a little.

2.

I'm having a hard time with my homework. I should...

Ⓐ sit and wait.

Ⓑ ask someone for help.

Ⓒ rip up my paper.

Name: _____ Date: _____

Dealing with Disappointment

It can be hard if you want something and you do not get it. It can make you mad at your family. But it can help to use self-talk. You can remind yourself of the things you do have. This will help you stay positive.

Directions: Match each example with the correct self-talk statement.

Focus on Family

Self-Awareness

Your sister won't play your favorite game with you.	"I know my parent still loves me."
Your parent won't buy you the toy you want.	"Maybe I can go to the movies next week."
Your grandparents can't take you to a movie.	"I can find another book to read."
Your brother won't let you borrow a book you want to read.	"Maybe my sister will play another game with me."

Name: _____ Date: _____

Focus on Family

Self-Management

Self-Control

It can be hard when you want something right away. You have to keep calm. Do not bubble up and explode like a volcano. It does not feel good. Be a problem-solver, and stay calm.

Directions: Next to the volcano, draw what your body does when you get angry. Next to the iceberg, draw what your body looks like when you stay calm.

Name: _____ Date: _____

Find Ways to Help Others

You may feel like you want to help someone. This is a great thing to do. Try to act on it as soon as you can.

Directions: Think about how you could help two people in your family. Finish the sentences.

Person 1 _____

Family Member: _____

This person likes _____

One kind thing I could do for them is _____

_____

Person 2 _____

Family Member: _____

This person likes _____

One kind thing I could do for them is _____

_____

Name: _____ Date: _____

Teamwork

Happy families work together. They help each other. You should do what you can to help.

Directions: Write who does each task in your family. Then, draw something you do to help your family.

Focus on Family

Relationship Skills

1. Who takes out the trash? _____

2. Who cleans the dishes? _____

3. Who makes dinner? _____

4. Who does laundry? _____

5. Who helps with homework? _____

Name: _____ Date: _____

Making Good Choices

You might make a choice that hurts someone in your family. If you do, you should try to help them feel better. You could make them something. You could say nice things to them.

Directions: Match what each person did to how they made things better.

Connie ate the last of her brother's cereal.	Use some money to help buy a new mirror.
Bree spilled juice on her sister's favorite shirt.	Help order a new remote.
Jake threw a ball and broke his mom's mirror.	Offer to help make his favorite breakfast.
Jerome stepped on the TV remote and broke it.	Wash the shirt.

Name: _____ Date: _____

Worry

To worry means you think of bad things that might happen. It is normal to worry. Some things will make you worry a little. Other things will make you worry a lot.

Directions: Write each worry on each line. On the top, write the things that worry you a lot. On the bottom, write the things that worry you a little.

getting hurt	making mistakes
getting into trouble	losing your friends
getting lost	making new friends

A Lot of Worry

A Little Worry

Name: _____ Date: _____

Deal with Worry

We all worry. It is normal to worry a little. You can learn how to relax.

Directions: Practice the ideas to calm your mind when you are worried. Then, draw a picture of the idea you like best.

Cool Your Cocoa

Hold your hands like you are holding cup of hot cocoa. Pretend you are blowing on it to cool it off. Take deep breaths, and blow slowly.

Move Your Body

Move your body. Get up and dance. Take five minutes, and shake it up!

Name: _____ Date: _____

Notice When Others Are Worried
Your friends have worries just like you do. You can tell when your friend is worried. But you need to pay attention.

Directions: Write how each person is showing they are worried.

1. Sylvia is worried about a piano lesson. How is she showing she is worried?

_____
_____
_____
_____
_____
_____

2. Charlie is worried about the big game. How is he showing he is worried?

_____
_____
_____
_____
_____
_____

Name: _____ Date: _____

Support Your Friends

You can help your friends when they are worried. You can help them feel better.

Directions: Write what you would say to help your friend. Then, draw a picture of how you would help your friend feel better.

Shaina is worried. She is changing schools and is afraid she won't have any friends.

_____

_____

_____

_____

_____

Name: _____ Date: _____

Focus on Friends

Responsible Decision-Making

Solve Problems

Problems with friends can make you worry. You can find ways to calm your mind when this happens. If you know what to do, you will feel better.

Directions: Circle the ideas that would help you calm your mind when you are worried. Then, draw your favorite idea.

Take a nap.	Read a book.
Listen to music.	Use self-talk.
Take deep breaths.	Go for a run.
Talk to a friend.	Count to 10.
Watch a show.	Color a picture.

Name: _____ Date: _____

Being Honest

Telling the truth can be hard when you think you might get in trouble. It feels better when you are honest. It takes time to build trust.

Directions: Read each example. Circle the honest choice.

1. Kiki was playing with a toy at a store. The toy broke.

2. Jonah is at church. He rips the page of a book.

3. Cam is at a movie theater. She spills her drink.

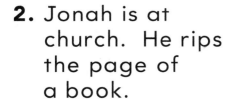

4. Jay is playing a game of dodgeball. He gets hit by the ball and is out.

Name: _____ Date: _____

Honesty and Kindness

Saying the first thing that comes to your mind is not always the kindest thing to say. It can help to stop and think about what you might say. Think about how your words might help or hurt other people.

Directions: Write something both honest and kind you could say to each person.

1. The librarian has some food in her teeth.

_____

_____

_____

_____

2. Your friend trips and falls in front of a lot of people.

_____

_____

_____

_____

3. Another person at a park is taking a long turn on a swing.

_____

_____

_____

_____

Noticing Dishonesty

People will say things that are not true. You can tell by what their bodies are doing.

Directions: Circle the part of each child's body that shows they are not telling the truth.

1. This child is having a hard time looking at the adult.

3. This child is fidgeting.

2. This child feels sick to his stomach.

4. This child is sweating.

Name: _____ Date: _____

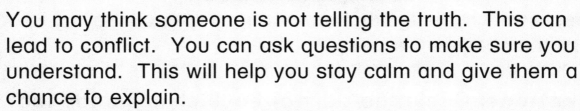

Communication

You may think someone is not telling the truth. This can lead to conflict. You can ask questions to make sure you understand. This will help you stay calm and give them a chance to explain.

Directions: Write questions you could ask to help you understand what you heard. Follow the example.

Example: You think you heard a teammate say that you are not good at dribbling.

Did you say something about me?

1. You think you heard your parents say that you were being mean to a friend.

_____

- - - - - - - - - - - - - - - - - - - -

_____

2. You think you heard a server at a restaurant say they dropped your food.

_____

- - - - - - - - - - - - - - - - - - - -

_____

3. You think you heard a friend say your shirt was ugly.

_____

- - - - - - - - - - - - - - - - - - - -

_____

Name: _____ Date: _____

Forgiveness

Sometimes, people you love will let you down. It will hurt your feelings. But you can forgive them. This can help build strong relationships.

Directions: Read the text. Answer the questions.

Jin's cousin said he was going to give him a present for his birthday. His cousin forgot.

1. What did Jin's cousin do?

_____

_____

_____

_____

_____

2. How does Jin feel?

_____

_____

_____

3. What could Jin do?

_____

_____

_____

_____

_____

_____

_____

Name: _____ Date: _____

Feelings Words

You have a lot of feelings. Knowing different feeling words will help you to say how you feel. This will help you deal with your feelings.

Directions: Use the Word Bank to write the words under the faces that match the feelings. Each face will have three words.

Word Bank		
angry	down	joyful
bummed	furious	mad
cheerful	happy	sad

_____ _____ _____

_____ _____ _____

_____ _____ _____

_____ _____ _____

Name: _____ Date: _____

Managing Stress

You will not always feel happy. Your body might feel tense.
You can feel less stressed by doing a body scan.

Directions: Follow the steps to do a body scan.
Then, rate how you feel.

Step 1: Find a quiet place to sit.

Step 2: Close your eyes.

Step 3: Spend five seconds
checking in to see
how each body part
feels: head, shoulders,
stomach, and legs.

Step 4: If one of these areas
feels tight, pause. Take
some deep breaths.

Step 5: Open your eyes. You are done.

Rate how you feel by coloring in a smiley face.

Self-Management

Focus on Self

Name: _____ Date: _____

Show Concern for Others

Sometimes, people we love will be sad. Or they will just have a bad day. You may not be able to fix what is making them sad. But you might be able to help cheer them up.

Directions: Find a friend, and read each other the jokes. Put a star by the one you like best. Then, answer the question.

1. What did the left eye say to the right eye?

   Between us, something smells.

2. What animal is always at a baseball game?

   a bat

3. Why can't Elsa have a balloon?

   Because she will "Let It Go."

4. Why was 6 afraid of 7?

   Because 7 8 9! (ate)

5. How else can you make someone laugh when they feel sad?

   _____

   _____

   _____

   _____

Name: _____ Date: _____

Help Others Feel Better

Friends won't always feel better right away. You may have to try more than one way to help.

Directions: Circle two ideas you could try the next time you see someone who is sad. Then, draw one of the ideas you circled.

Name: _____ Date: _____

Reflect about Your Friends

Who helps you feel better when you are sad? It feels good to have people around you who help you feel better!

Directions: Draw a time when you were sad. Include who was there with you. Then, answer the questions.

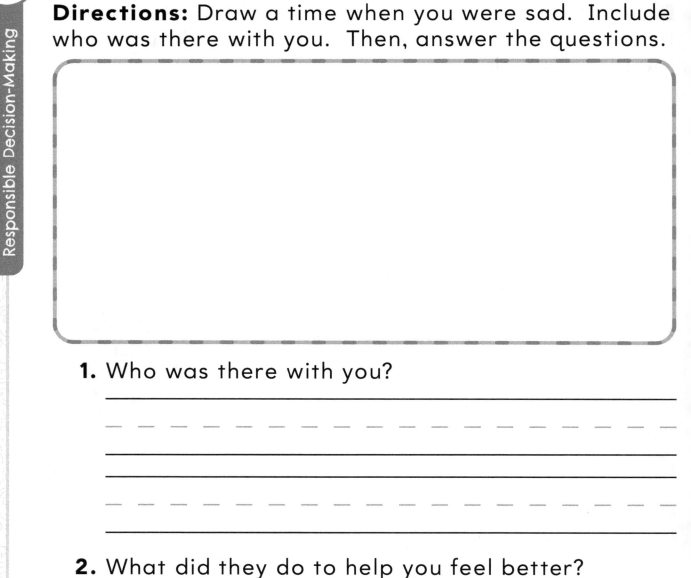

1. Who was there with you?

_____

_ _

_____

_ _

_____

2. What did they do to help you feel better?

_____

_ _

_____

_ _

_____

Identity

The place you are from is part of your identity. Your neighborhood helps make you who you are.

Directions: Design a T-shirt for your neighborhood. Use some of the ideas in the box, or use your own.

the name of your town or city	your neighbors
things you like to do there	your favorite restaurant
	your favorite shop
your family	your favorite place to play

Focus on Neighborhood

Self-Awareness

Name: _____ Date: _____

Focus on Neighborhood

Self-Management

Bravery

Neighbors can also be friends. It takes bravery to meet new friends. But it is worth it.

Directions: Draw a picture of your neighborhood. Draw and label the people you know.

Name: _____ Date: _____

Working Together

Neighbors work together. They help people who live there stay safe. Teamwork makes people feel good.

Directions: Write how each neighborhood could make things better.

1. _____
_____
_____
_____
_____
_____

2. _____
_____
_____
_____
_____
_____

3. _____
_____
_____
_____
_____
_____

Name: _____ Date: _____

Caring for Others

Your neighborhood is a better place when people help each other. This helps keep you safe. And it keeps your neighbors safe, too.

Directions: Draw yourself doing each of these things to help your neighbors.

1. You see a neighbor fall off their bike.

2. A neighbor spills groceries on the ground.

Name: _____ Date: _____

Dealing with Change

Your neighborhood will change over time. You could get a new school or a new playground. Neighborhoods often have to ask for these new things.

Directions: Read the story. Then, write who each person talks to.

Fixing the School

Nina saw that her school was starting to look old. There were cracks in the walls. The tiles on the floor were dirty. And there were not enough bathrooms for all the students. She talked to her teacher. Her teacher talked to the principal. The principal talked to the school board. The school board talked to the city. The city had the community vote. The community voted to fix the school.

_____

Nina talks to her _____,

who talks to the _____,

who talks to the _____,

who talks to the _____,

who has people vote.

Name: _____ Date: _____

Stand Up for Yourself

Your feelings and needs are important. You will need to stand up for yourself. You can do this by clearly telling people what you need.

Directions: Write what each person can say to stand up for themselves.

1.

_____

- -

_____

_____

- -

_____

2.

This math is hard.

_____

- -

_____

_____

- -

_____

Name: _____ Date: _____

Set Goals

Practice will help you improve. The more you practice, the better you will become. This can be hard. It takes time and effort.

Directions: Circle one thing you would like to do better. Write how you can improve.

What could you do to improve?

_____

1. _____

_____

_____

2. _____

_____

_____

Name: _____ Date: _____

Empathy

Empathy means you understand how someone is feeling. This will help you know how they feel. Then, you can help them feel better.

Directions: Imagine your friend is sad that she has to move to a new school. She is afraid her teacher won't like her. Write her a letter showing empathy. Then, draw a picture to help her feel better.

_____

- -

_____

- -

_____

- -

_____

- -

_____

Apologies

Sometimes, you will hurt a friend's feelings. It is good to find a way to make things better. You will make better friends.

Directions: Write an apology for each picture. Write what you are sorry for. Offer to make things better.

1. _____

_____

_____

2. _____

_____

_____

Name: _____ Date: _____

Make Safe Choices

It is important to make safe choices at school. That will keep you and your friends safe.

Directions: List things that are safe to do at school. List things that are not safe to do at school. Draw one of the safe choices.

Safe	Not Safe

Focus on School

Responsible Decision-Making

Name: _____ Date: _____

Role Models

A role model is someone you can act like. You study what they do. Then, you do it yourself.

Directions: Draw someone who you want to act like. It could be someone you know, such as a parent or a coach. Or it could be a famous person. Then, answer the question.

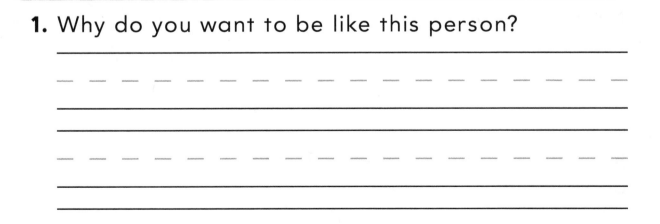

1. Why do you want to be like this person?

_____

_____

_____

_____

Focus on Community

Self-Awareness

Name: _____ Date: _____

Managing Stress

When you get too busy, you can feel stressed. It's good to have a few ways to cool down.

Directions: Follow along with this breathing activity.

Step 1: Imagine you have a bowl of hot soup in your hands.

Step 2: Smell your soup as you count 1, 2, 3, 4, 5.

Step 3: The soup is hot! Blow on the soup as you count 1, 2, 3, 4, 5.

Step 4: Do you feel calm? If not, do it again.

Benefits of Your Community

Your community has a lot of things to do. Some of those things are really fun. They are even more fun with friends.

Directions: Pretend a new kid has moved in to your community. Draw three fun things you would want to do with them.

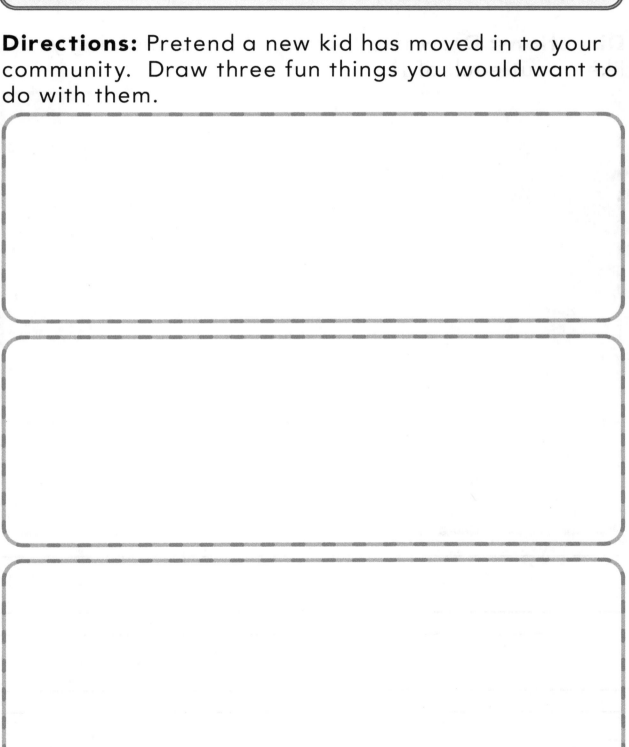

Name: _____ Date: _____

Make Good Friends

People may hurt your feelings. It helps to remember what you like about them. This will help you forgive them.

Directions: Draw two friends. Write something you like about each of them.

_____   _____
- - - - - - - - - - - - - - -   - - - - - - - - - - - - - - -
_____   _____
- - - - - - - - - - - - - - -   - - - - - - - - - - - - - - -
_____   _____
- - - - - - - - - - - - - - -   - - - - - - - - - - - - - - -
_____   _____

Small and Big Problems

Remember, you can solve small problems on your own. You need an adult to help you solve big problems. It can be hard to know if a problem is big or small.

Directions: Draw a line from the picture to the size of the problem.

Small Problem	Big Problem

Focus on Community

Responsible Decision-Making

Name: _____ Date: _____

Use a Mantra

You can use a mantra to get through hard times. This is a short phrase you say every day. It will remind you of how great you are.

Directions: Color one of the mantras you like. Say it to yourself several times to see if it feels good.

I am loved.	I matter.	Everything will be okay.
I am important.	I get better every day.	I deserve to be happy.
I can take it one step at a time.	I forgive myself for my mistakes.	I can make a difference.

Directions: Write the mantra you chose in the box, and decorate it.

Name: _____ Date: _____

Accepting a Loss

It can be hard to lose. Learning how to be a good sport when you lose will make you feel better.

Directions: Dan's team just lost a game. Write three things he and his teammates can do to be good sports.

_____

1. _____

_____

2. _____

_____

3. _____

Directions: Draw how it will feel when they are good sports about their loss.

Name: _____ Date: _____

Focus on Self

Social Awareness

Point of View

People have different views. This means they think differently. And that's a good thing. Life is more fun when there is more than one side to a story. If you have a conflict, think about the other person's point of view. This will help you solve it.

Directions: Read the text. Answer the questions.

Dev wants to paint. Rick wants to play dinosaurs. Both Dev and Rick want to use the table for their activities.

1. What does Dev want? _____
_____
_____
_____

2. What does Rick want? _____
_____
_____
_____

3. Write one solution. _____
_____
_____
_____

126957—180 Days of Social-Emotional Learning

© Shell Education

Name: _____ Date: _____

Listening Skills

Listening skills will help you learn. They will help you be a better friend, too. With two ears and one mouth, we should try to listen twice as much as we talk.

Directions: Color the pictures as you read each skill. Draw a star by the listening skill that you do well. Circle the skill that is hard for you to do. Draw a square around the listening skill that you will try today.

1. Look at the speaker.

2. Keep your body still.

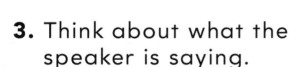

3. Think about what the speaker is saying.

4. Ask questions if you are confused.

Name: _____ Date: _____

Critical Thinking

Critical thinking is careful thinking. It means thinking about a problem in a new way. It can take a lot of work. But it can lead to the best solution. Slow down to think. Sometimes, it can help to think about what your role model would do.

Directions: Study the pictures. Write what you think your role model would do.

1. _____

_____

_____

_____

2. _____

_____

_____

_____

Name: _____ Date: _____

Your Impact

The way you act can make others feel happy or sad.

Directions: Write how each person's actions will make others feel.

1. Lily made cookies for her new neighbors. How would this make Lily's neighbors feel?

_____

- - - - - - - - - - - - - - - - - -

_____

2. Phil offers to walk his neighbor's dog. How would this make Phil's neighbor feel?

_____

- - - - - - - - - - - - - - - - - -

_____

3. Manny offers to help a neighbor rake some leaves. How would this make Manny's neighbor feel?

_____

- - - - - - - - - - - - - - - - - -

_____

4. Stella takes her neighbor's new scooter. How would this make Stella's neighbor feel?

_____

- - - - - - - - - - - - - - - - - -

_____

Name: _____ Date: _____

Choose Kindness

Be kind when you can. Being kind feels good for you and for others.

Directions: Draw the kind thing to do for each example.

1. Franny sees Kale's football in her yard.

2. Milo sees money fall out of a neighbor's pocket.

3. Alice sees a kid trip and fall.

Name: _____ Date: _____

Different Rules

Every place has its own set of rules. You have to learn to stay safe in different places.

Directions: Write a rule for each place.

1. _____
_____
_____

2. _____
_____
_____

3. _____
_____
_____

4. _____
_____
_____

Name: _____ Date: _____

Problem-Solving

Friends can have conflicts. You can become better friends when you work through conflicts.

Directions: Write how each set of friends could solve their problem together.

1. Two friends both want to go down the slide at the park.

_____

- - - - - - - - - - - - - - -

_____

_____

- - - - - - - - - - - - - - -

_____

2. Two friends both want to play with the basketball.

_____

- - - - - - - - - - - - - - -

_____

_____

- - - - - - - - - - - - - - -

_____

Name: _____ Date: _____

Impact of Your Choices

What you say and how you act can change how others feel. When you are nice, people feel good. When you are mean, people feel bad.

Directions: Draw what you think will happen next.

1.

2.

3.

4.

Name: _____ Date: _____

The Power of *Yet*

The word *yet* is very powerful. If you think you can't do something, you won't do it. You are less likely to try it again. If you think you can't do it *yet*, you might try again. You will feel more positive. You are more likely to succeed.

Directions: Write three things you know how to do above the word *yet*. Write things you can't do yet below the word.

Name: _____ Date: _____

Use *Yet* to Set Goals

Use the power of *yet* to help you reach your school goals. Focus on getting better. Learn new things. Then, you will be able to push through when things get tough.

Focus on School

Self-Management

Directions: Write something you want to learn. Then, draw a comic of you getting better at it.

Goal: I want to learn how to...

_____

- -

_____

_____

I can't do _____ YET.

I am getting better.

I can do it!

Name: _____ Date: _____

Use *Yet* to See Others' Strengths

You can help your friends see what they can do by using the power of *yet*. You can encourage your friends to keep going. They can learn. They just aren't there yet.

Directions: Write what you could say to help each of these friends. Use the power of *yet*. Then, draw how they would feel after you help them.

1. Felicia is having a hard time reading out loud. She gets really frustrated.

_____

_____

_____

2. Molly is angry that she isn't starting in a basketball game. Her coach tells her to work on her free throws.

_____

_____

_____

Name: _____ Date: _____

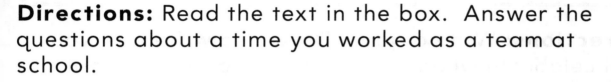

Use *Yet* to Work Together

Working with others on something you can't do yet can be very powerful. It helps you grow. It helps them grow, too.

Directions: Read the text in the box. Answer the questions about a time you worked as a team at school.

Benefits of Working as a Team

You get to use each other's strengths.

You build trust in each other.

You build stronger friendships.

You feel good about doing something together.

---

1. What did you work to achieve?

_____

- -

_____

_____

- -

_____

2. How did you feel?

_____

- -

_____

_____

- -

_____

Name: _____ Date: _____

Focus on School

Responsible Decision-Making

Celebrate Your Success

When you reach a goal, it is good to celebrate. You earned it. It can help to imagine how you will celebrate as you work toward a goal.

Directions: Write a goal. Draw and write how you will celebrate when you reach your goal at school.

_____

My goal: _____

Your Gift to the Community

You have worked hard this year. Now, you can use your skills to make your community a better place.

Directions: Underline the skills you are the best at.

being brave

being honest

being mindful

calming down

communicating

controlling your emotions

knowing your feelings

making good friends

problem-solving

setting goals

staying organized

thinking about others

working on a team

Directions: Draw yourself using one of these skills in your community.

Name: _____ Date: _____

Setting Goals

It is important to work hard at things you do not yet know how to do. It can help to make a plan to improve.

Directions: Draw a star by at least one thing you think you could do better. Then, answer the questions.

being honest	making good friends
being mindful	problem-solving
communicating well	setting goals
controlling your emotions	staying organized
	thinking about others
knowing your feelings	working on a team

1. How can you practice this skill?

_____

_ _ _ _ _ _ _ _ _ _ _ _ _ _ _ _ _ _

_____

2. Who can you practice with?

_____

_ _ _ _ _ _ _ _ _ _ _ _ _ _ _ _ _ _

_____

3. How long do you think it will take to get better?

_____

_ _ _ _ _ _ _ _ _ _ _ _ _ _ _ _ _ _

_____

Name: _____ Date: _____

Be Grateful

There are a lot of people in your community who help you. There are also a lot of ways to thank those people. One way is to write a note.

Directions: Design a card to say thank you to someone who has helped you. Be specific about what the person has done to help.

Focus on Community

Social Awareness

Name: _____ Date: _____

Be a Leader

You have worked to improve your skills this year. It's time to put all the hard work you have done to good use.

Focus on Community

Relationship Skills

Directions: Help solve each of these problems.

1. Both students want to sit in the same chair. How could you help?

_____

_____

_____

_____

_____

2. This student is being unsafe. What could you say?

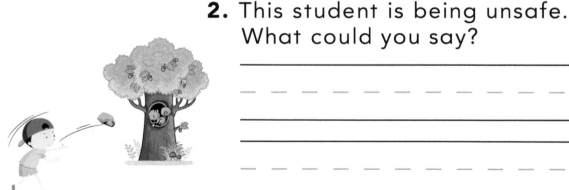

_____

_____

_____

_____

_____

3. This boy didn't make a team. He is sad. How could you help?

_____

_____

_____

_____

_____

Name: _____ Date: _____

Being Proud

It's good to stop and think about all the things you are proud of. You have grown so much.

Directions: Write something you have done that you are proud of on each leaf.

Answer Key

There are many open-ended pages and writing prompts in this book. For these activities, the answers will vary. Examples are given as needed.

Week 1 Day 1 (page 12)

1. sad
2. happy
3. scared
4. angry

Week 1 Day 3 (page 14)

From top to bottom: scared, happy, angry, sad

Week 1 Day 4 (page 15)

The pictures of a child helping with homework and sharing their lunch should be circled.

Week 2 Day 4 (page 20)

Pick up your toys: second picture
Push in your chair: fourth picture
Close your door: first picture
Brush your teeth: third picture

Week 2 Day 5 (page 21)

1. Pictures may include Matt talking to an adult or asking his sister to stop.
2. Pictures may include Margo helping her mom clean up or getting a towel for her mom.
3. Pictures may include Jack talking to his brother or asking for help from his parents.

Week 3 Day 3 (page 24)

1. One friend is being left out of a game.
2. She is feeling lonely, sad, or left out.

Week 3 Day 4 (page 25)

1. Pictures may include a student picking up trash.
2. Pictures may include a student helping to fix the tire or going to find help.

Week 3 Day 5 (page 26)

1. big problem
2. small problem
3. big problem
4. small problem

Week 4 Day 2 (page 28)

1. Color the picture of a student taking a deep breath.
2. Color the picture of a student taking a deep breath.

Week 5 Day 1 (page 32)

1. sad
2. scared
3. angry
4. love

Week 5 Day 4 (page 35)

1. scared; circle hands and face
2. happy; circle arms, hands, and face

Week 5 Day 5 (page 36)

Pictures may include students sharing the paints and brushes or taking turns.

Week 6 Day 1 (page 37)

Examples:
1. I broke the flower pot. I'm sorry.
2. I knocked over your garbage can. I'm sorry.
3. I broke your window. I'm sorry.

Week 6 Day 2 (page 38)

1. The cars are driving too fast. People may get hurt.
2. The singer is keeping the neighbor awake at night.
3. There is too much trash in the park.

Week 6 Day 3 (page 39)

1. Thank you for helping me put air in my bike tire.
2. Thank you for playing soccer with me.
3. Thank you for pushing me on the swing.

Week 6 Day 5 (page 41)

Examples:
1. The toy might break.
2. They could both have fun with the toy. They would both be happy.

Answer Key *(cont.)*

Week 7 Day 2 (page 43)

Examples:

1. We are playing basketball. Please leave us alone.
2. We are going to finish our game. Then, the court is all yours.

Week 7 Day 4 (page 45)

Examples:

1. Ask them to play a game with you.
2. Ask them to eat next to you at lunch.

Week 7 Day 5 (page 46)

1. Answers may include: listen to adults, clean up after myself, and be kind to others.

Week 8 Day 2 (page 48)

Examples:

1. Let me help you up. Would you like to come play with me?
2. Do you want someone to play with today?
3. It's not kind to make fun of other people.

Week 8 Day 3 (page 49)

Library: climbing on the shelves, hitting
Pool: pushing, diving into the shallow end

Week 8 Day 4 (page 50)

From top to bottom: That's stealing. I won't do that; It's not nice to make fun of people; You should not hurt people; We should not break things.

Week 9 Day 5 (page 56)

Examples:

1. They could play rock, paper, scissors to decide who goes first.
2. One of them could go first. Then, they could switch for the next game.

Week 10 Day 1 (page 57)

From top to bottom: I'm sorry. I knocked over the beads; I'm sorry. I threw the ball and broke the vase; I'm sorry. I ate the cake.

Week 10 Day 4 (page 60)

Examples:

1. Can you please help me tie my shoes?
2. Can you please help me get the milk?
3. Can you please help me with my homework?

Week 10 Day 5 (page 61)

1. good
2. good
3. bad
4. bad

Week 11 Day 3 (page 64)

1. angry
2. scared
3. grateful

Week 11 Day 5 (page 66)

Play with the ball together.
Tell an adult, and try to make it better.

Week 12 Day 1 (page 67)

From top to bottom: food pantry, fire station, hospital

Week 12 Day 3 (page 69)

Examples:

1. The sign keeps me safe from cars driving by.
2. I might get hurt if I'm too small.
3. No, it is not fair. Girls should be able to go where boys do.

Week 12 Day 4 (page 70)

1. reading a book
2. playing basketball
3. taking a walk

Week 14 Day 1 (page 77)

1. scared
2. shy
3. excited
4. angry

Week 14 Day 2 (page 78)

From top to bottom: I'm sad we lost. It was really fun to play in the game; The library will be open another day; I don't like waiting. But it won't be too long; I'll be okay. There is other food I like.

Week 14 Day 4 (page 80)

From top to bottom: Kids play in the street in your neighborhood; There is a crosswalk on a busy street; A new home is being built on your road; People have seen bears in your neighborhood.

Answer Key (cont.)

Week 15 Day 3 (page 84)
Examples:
1. I could help her pick up the backpack.
2. I could invite her to play.

Week 15 Day 5 (page 86)
Big Problems: You see smoke coming from a computer; Mayra falls and breaks her foot; Julio takes food from your lunch.

Small Problems: Ron takes your pencil; Aimee is thirsty.

Week 16 Day 2 (page 88)
Examples:
Boy—Eyes: closed; Mouth: open, teeth clenched; Hands: on head, pulling hair
Girl—Eyes: watery; Mouth: closed; Hands: on mouth

Week 16 Day 5 (page 91)
1. calm
2. stressed

Week 17 Day 3 (page 94)
Examples:
1. Thank you for helping me clean up.
2. Thank you for asking me to play.

Week 18 Day 2 (page 98)
Examples:
1. It will feel good to get my room clean.
2. This looks hard, but I can do it.
3. This will not take that long.

Week 18 Day 4 (page 100)
1. sweeping or cleaning
2. making their bed
3. mowing the lawn

Week 19 Day 1 (page 102)
Examples:
1. sad
2. angry
3. disappointed

Week 19 Day 2 (page 103)
1. B
2. A

Week 19 Day 3 (page 104)
Examples:
1. embarrassed that he lost control
2. angry that he fell
3. angry that her friend thinks she cheated
4. upset that she lost

Week 19 Day 4 (page 105)
Examples:
I feel mad when you steal my snack. Next time, will you please ask me first?
I feel angry when you rip my picture. Next time, will you please be more careful?

Week 19 Day 5 (page 106)
1. no
2. yes
3. yes
4. no

Week 20 Day 1 (page 107)
1. They are blushing and frowning.
2. She is blushing, and her hand is over her mouth.

Week 20 Day 2 (page 108)
From top to bottom:
Can you teach me how to tie my shoes?
Can you show me how to hit the tennis ball?
Can you help me find a book about bears?
Can you help me learn how to make a basket?

Week 20 Day 4 (page 110)
1. They are helping a student with a problem.
2. They are keeping people safe in the water.
3. They are helping someone with their helmet.

Week 20 Day 5 (page 111)
1. people not wearing seatbelts
2. keeping me safe in a car crash
3. pushing people into the pool
4. keeping me from falling in water

Week 21 Day 3 (page 114)
From top to bottom: Nice game. Let's play again; What you said really hurt my feelings; Delete and ignore messages from strangers.

Answer Key *(cont.)*

Week 21 Day 4 (page 115)

1. laugh out loud
2. be right back
3. I'm laughing.
4. I'm sad.

Week 21 Day 5 (page 116)

Spilling water may break the computer.

Week 22 Day 5 (page 121)

taking your toy; breaking your window

Week 23 Day 3 (page 124)

Examples:

1. sad
2. Help them study. Tell them it's just one test. They'll do better next time.
3. angry
4. Help them make something new.

Week 23 Day 4 (page 125)

Example: I'm sorry I spilled paint on your painting. Can I help you clean it up?

Week 23 Day 5 (page 126)

Big Problems: I lost my book; I fell and hurt my arm.

Small Problems: I can't find my pencil; My friend tripped me; My friend is teasing me; I lost a game; I ripped my paper; I don't feel like singing.

Week 24 Day 1 (page 127)

1. scared; sad; shy
2. She is hiding behind the adult.
3. happy
4. She is smiling.

Week 24 Day 4 (page 130)

1. Ed is not allowed to dance because he is a boy.
2. Example: Ed should be allowed to dance. He's really good, and he loves doing it.

Week 24 Day 5 (page 131)

1. He is helping people recycle.
2. She is giving shoes to kids in need.

Week 25 Day 5 (page 136)

1. C
2. B

Week 26 Day 1 (page 137)

From top to bottom: Maybe my sister will play another game with me; I know my parent still loves me; Maybe I can go to the movies next week; I can find another book to read.

Week 26 Day 5 (page 141)

From top to bottom: Offer to help make his favorite breakfast; Wash the shirt; Use some money to help buy a new mirror; Help order a new remote.

Week 27 Day 3 (page 144)

1. Sylvia is biting her nails.
2. Charlie is holding his stomach.

Week 28 Day 1 (page 147)

1. The second picture should be circled.
2. The first picture should be circled.
3. The first picture should be circled.
4. The second picture should be circled.

Week 28 Day 2 (page 148)

Examples:

1. Excuse me, you have a little food in your teeth.
2. Are you ok? I'm so sorry that happened.
3. Is it alright if I have a turn?

Week 28 Day 3 (page 149)

1. The eyes should be circled.
2. The stomach should be circled.
3. The hand should be circled.
4. The face should be circled.

Week 28 Day 4 (page 150)

Examples:

1. Did you say something about me?
2. Did you say you dropped my food?
3. Did you say something about my shirt?

Week 28 Day 5 (page 151)

Examples:

1. Jin's cousin didn't bring a present.
2. Jin is upset.
3. Jin could tell himself that he does not need presents.

Answer Key (cont.)

Week 29 Day 1 (page 152)

Happy face: happy, joyful, cheerful
Sad face: sad, down, bummed
Angry face: mad, furious, angry

Week 30 Day 3 (page 159)

Examples:

1. The neighborhood could clean up the trash.
2. The neighborhood could help clean up the spray paint.
3. The neighborhood could raise money to fix the court.

Week 30 Day 5 (page 161)

teacher; principal; school board; city

Week 31 Day 1 (page 162)

1. It's not funny to make fun of people. Stop laughing at me.
2. I don't understand. Can you go over that again?

Week 31 Day 2 (page 163)

Examples:

1. I could practice.
2. I could find a friend to help me.

Week 31 Day 4 (page 165)

1. I'm sorry I broke your pencil. Can I find you a new one?
2. I'm sorry I knocked you down. Can I help you to the nurse?

Week 32 Day 5 (page 171)

Small Problems: Waiting in line, broken pencil, looking for something

Big Problems: Spilling food, lost in a parking lot, getting hurt in a game

Week 33 Day 2 (page 173)

Examples: They could shake hands, tell the other team they did a good job, or compliment someone on a good play they made.

Week 33 Day 3 (page 174)

1. Dev wants to paint on the table.
2. Rick wants to set up his dinosaurs on the table.
3. Example: Dev could use part of the table to paint, and Rick could use the other part.

Week 34 Day 1 (page 177)

Examples:

1. The cookies would make them feel happy and welcomed.
2. Walking the dog would make them feel happy and grateful.
3. Raking leaves would make them feel grateful.
4. Taking the scooter would make them feel angry.

Week 34 Day 3 (page 179)

Examples:

1. Watch out for cars.
2. Don't throw food.
3. Stay with an adult.
4. Don't hide in the racks.

Week 34 Day 4 (page 180)

Examples:

1. They could play rock, paper, scissors to see who goes down the slide first.
2. They could play basketball together.

Week 35 Day 3 (page 184)

Examples:

1. You just can't read yet. You'll get better!
2. You are getting better at your free throws. You just can't make them yet. Keep practicing, and you will get them.

Week 36 Day 4 (page 190)

Examples:

1. Suggest that they could play rock, paper, scissors to see who gets to sit in the seat.
2. Say it is not nice to be mean to animals, and ask them to stop.
3. Tell him to keep practicing and maybe try making another team.

References Cited

The Aspen Institute: National Commission on Social, Emotional, & Academic Development. 2018. "From a Nation at Risk to a Nation at Hope." https://nationathope.org/wp-content/uploads/2018_aspen_final-report_full_webversion.pdf.

Collaborative for Academic, Social, and Emotional Learning (CASEL). n.d. "What Is SEL?" Last modified December 2020. https://casel.org/what-is-sel/.

Durlak, Joseph A., Roger P. Weissberg, Allison B. Dymnicki, Rebecca D. Taylor, and Kriston B. Schellinger. 2011. "The Impact of Enhancing Students' Social and Emotional Learning: A Meta-Analysis of School-Based Universal Interventions." *Child Development* 82 (1): 405–32.

Goleman, Daniel. 2005. *Emotional Intelligence: Why It Can Matter More Than IQ.* New York: Bantam Dell.

Palmer, Parker J. 2007. *The Courage to Teach: Exploring the Inner Landscape of a Teacher's Life.* San Francisco: Jossey-Bass.

Name: _____ Date: _____

Connecting to Self Rubric

Days 1 and 2

Directions: Complete this rubric every six weeks to evaluate students' Day 1 and Day 2 activity sheets. Only one rubric is needed per student. Their work over the six weeks can be considered together. Appraise their work in each category by circling or highlighting the descriptor in each row that best describes the student's work. Then, consider the student's overall progress in connecting to self. In the box, draw ☆, ✓+ , or ✓ to indicate your overall evaluation.

Competency	Advanced	Satisfactory	Developing
Self-Awareness	Can accurately identify one's own full range of emotions.	Identifies one's own emotions accurately most of the time.	Has trouble identifying their own feelings.
	Understands that thoughts and feelings are connected.	Sees the connection of thoughts and feelings most of the time.	Does not connect thoughts to feelings.
	Can identify strengths and areas of growth.	Can identify a few strengths and weaknesses.	Can identify only one strength or weakness.
Self-Management	Can manage stress by using several different strategies.	Manages stress with only one strategy.	Does not manage stress well.
	Shows motivation in all areas of learning.	Shows motivation in a few areas of learning.	Shows little to no motivation.
	Is able to set realistic goals.	Sets some goals that are realistic and some that are not.	Has a hard time setting goals that are achievable.

Comments

_____

_____

_____

_____

Overall

[ ]

Name: _____ Date: _____

Relating to Others Rubric

Days 3 and 4

Directions: Complete this rubric every six weeks to evaluate students' Day 3 and Day 4 activity sheets. Only one rubric is needed per student. Their work over the six weeks can be considered together. Appraise their work in each category by circling or highlighting the descriptor in each row that best describes the student's work. Then, consider the student's overall progress in relating to others. In the box, draw ☆, ✓+ , or ✓ to indicate your overall evaluation.

Competency	Advanced	Satisfactory	Developing
Social Awareness	Shows empathy toward others.	Shows empathy toward others most of the time.	Shows little to no empathy toward others.
	Can explain how rules are different in different places.	Knows that some places can have different rules.	Is not able to articulate how rules may change in different places.
	Can list many people who support them in their learning.	Can list some people who support them in their learning.	Can list few people who support them in their learning.
Relationship Skills	Uses a variety of strategies to solve conflicts with peers.	Has a few strategies to solve conflicts with peers.	Struggles to solve conflicts with peers.
	Uses advanced skills of listening and paraphrasing while communicating.	Is able to communicate effectively.	Has breakdowns in communication skills.
	Works effectively with a team. Shows leadership in accomplishing team goals.	Works effectively with a team most of the time.	Has trouble working with others on a team.

Comments

Overall

_____

_____

_____

_____

Name: _____ Date: _____

Making Decisions Rubric

Day 5

Directions: Complete this rubric every six weeks to evaluate students' Day 5 activity sheets. Only one rubric is needed per student. Their work over the six weeks can be considered together. Appraise their work in each category by circling or highlighting the descriptor in each row that best describes the student's work. Then, consider the student's overall progress in making decisions. In the box, draw ☆, ✓+, or ✓ to indicate your overall evaluation.

Competency	Advanced	Satisfactory	Developing
Responsible Decision-Making	Makes decisions that benefit their own long-term interests.	Makes decisions that are sometimes impulsive and sometimes thought out.	Is impulsive and has a hard time making constructive choices.
	Knows how to keep self and others safe in a variety of situations.	Knows how to keep themselves safe in most situations.	Is capable of being safe, but sometimes is not.
	Is able to consider the consequences of their actions, both good and bad.	Is able to identify some consequences of their actions.	Struggles to anticipate possible consequences to their actions.

Comments

_____

_____

_____

_____

Overall

[ ]

Connecting to Self Analysis

Directions: Record each student's overall symbols (page 198) in the appropriate columns. At a glance, you can view: (1) which students need more help mastering these skills and (2) how students progress throughout the school year.

Student Name	Week 6	Week 12	Week 18	Week 24	Week 30	Week 36

Relating to Others Analysis

Directions: Record each student's overall symbols (page 199) in the appropriate columns. At a glance, you can view: (1) which students need more help mastering these skills and (2) how students progress throughout the school year.

Student Name	Week 6	Week 12	Week 18	Week 24	Week 30	Week 36

Making Decisions Analysis

Directions: Record each student's overall symbols (page 200) in the appropriate columns. At a glance, you can view: (1) which students need more help mastering these skills and (2) how students progress throughout the school year.

Student Name	Week 6	Week 12	Week 18	Week 24	Week 30	Week 36

Digital Resources

Accessing the Digital Resources

The Digital Resources can be downloaded by following these steps:

1. Go to **www.tcmpub.com/digital**

2. Use the ISBN number to redeem the Digital Resources.

3. Respond to the question using the book.

4. Follow the prompts on the Content Cloud website to sign in or create a new account.

5. Choose the Digital Resources you would like to download. You can download all the files at once, or a specific group of files.

ISBN:
9781087649702